Doris Marshall-Slack

PERSEVERANCE LANE
A Teacher's Story

Doris L. Marshall-Slack

Noble House
Baltimore, Maryland

PERSEVERANCE LANE

Library of Congress
Cataloging-in-Publication Data
ISBN 1-56167-854-6

Library of Congress Card Catalog Number:
2004091982

Published by

8019 Belair Road, Suite 10
Baltimore, Maryland 21236

Manufactured in the United States of America

This book is dedicated to the memory of my mother, Ludie Winston-Hill, and to my children, William Jr., David, Gregory, Patrick, Doris Jean, and Shawny. A special thanks goes to my two eldest sons, William Jr. and David who made a great contribution to my getting a college education; and to my dear friend, Rosie Shannon who encouraged me immensely down through the years. This book is also dedicated to all people who think they cannot make it because life has thrown them a curve.

Ludie Winston-Hill

LIFE

My high school days were happy days
Filled with laughter and cheer
I was old enough to enjoy life
Young enough to be of cares free
It was said by a former teacher
That we were going over fool's hill

Maturity was just over the hill
I like to recall foolish days
And remember a wise old teacher
Christmas always meant cheer
Easter meant setting us free
Spring always gave us more life

But for us there would be no life
Had the Savior not gone to Golgotha's hill
And gave his life for us to be free
He abolished bondage days
For unhappiness he gave us cheer
I'm speaking of the world's most famous teacher

Of course no one else can replace this teacher
Nor to us give life
No other shall bring such cheer
Nor dare to climb that hill
Who else can be dead for three days
And then from the grave be free

Man's soul is now free
He's had the best teacher
We've had many happy days
Our intent is to enjoy life
My journey is now completed over fool's hill
It is indeed a time for cheer

The happiness of my children fills me with cheer
They remind me of birds that are free
My reflection is now going over fool's hill
Hopefully they too will appreciate the best teacher
There is a time in each life
That's filled with carefree days

If you've lived you've had a teacher
For a teacher is life
Where wisdom increases with the days

— Doris L. Marshall-Slack

LOVE IS AN INSANITY

Love is an insanity
That possesses the heart, mind, and will
Love is that strong, strong force
That leads one's inner self into captivity

I found my true love
At a most inopportune time
There's an approach-avoidance conflict within
That's destroying my inner self

I have a deep desire to be with my love
To share in the giving and receiving of love
But if I follow my heart
I shudder to think where it may lead me

It is indeed true
That the eyes are the mirrors of the soul
Yet looking into your eyes
I see no reflection of what's in your heart

I am now helplessly, hopelessly in love
Oh how I long
To escape this insanity
This sweet, sweet misery

And darling, if I should choose
To follow my head
Please be assured
That it's only because I think it's best

But if the time should come
When you need me
Just call and I'll be there
Though I risk losing the love and respect
Of others near and dear to me
If you should ever need me
Call, darling, and I shall be there.

—Doris L. Marshall-Slack

Contents

INTRODUCTION

This is the unforgettable, eternal story of an African American female's struggle from the pits of poverty to a ray of sunshine at the top of life's hill. It tells of a young girl's experiences in the south during Jim Crow days, years before the Civil Rights Movement began. The protagonist describes what life was like for her as the product of a broken home and a dysfunctional marriage. She reveals what she encountered when she returned to high school to pursue a diploma and then entered the university where she earned a Bachelors Degree in Speech Communication, and later a Masters Degree in Education. This was all done against the wishes of her husband. The protagonist describes what life was like for her as a wife, mother, student, and teacher. She stresses the importance of getting a grip on life and surviving against the odds.

Perseverance Lane is filled with pathos because it deals with human emotions. This story will evoke within its readers feelings of pity, anger, laughter, sadness, and admiration. The protagonist conveys to the reader how faith in God and a strong determination helped her to persevere and achieve within an academic world that was alien to her limited experience. In the final chapter, the author pays tribute to her deceased mother who she referred to as "a wonderful person, and a great role model." Also, the protagonist discusses her outlook on life after receiving the news that her second born son, David, was terminally ill.

No one who reads *Perseverance Lane* will ever forget it, and many readers will never be quite the same after having read this book. Readers who learn from the mistakes of various characters within this story and embrace the positive attributes of this book shall emerge from its pages as the beneficiaries.

CHAPTER 1

Chapter 1

My sister, brother, and I went to the funeral home recently to view our mother's body. We had to be sure her body was ready for viewing by the general public. She lay there in her casket looking as if she weighed no more than a hundred pounds. I realized that I had lost my best friend. I was reminded of my humble beginning.

I was born Perseverance Lane in the rural area of Warrington, Tennessee. I am the third of four daughters born to Ludie and Harvey Lane. We lived on my grandfather Gene's farm. My paternal grandparents lived in the big house on the farm. It was bottom land that was separated from the rest of the surrounding community by a large creek which would sometimes overflow. If the water was moderately high, and we had someplace to go, Daddy would put on his hip boots and carry us across individually.

As I look back, I realize that those were the happiest, most secure days of my childhood. It meant a lot to my sisters and me to live in our own home with our mother and father. I thought of the fun Mona, Lila, and I used to have making mud pies and playing games while living in that little house in the bottom in Tennessee. Our favorite game was putting chickens to sleep. Each one of us would have one of Daddy's empty little tobacco sacks. We would fill it with dirt, lay the chicken on its side with its head on the bag of dirt, as if it were a pillow. We would then rub the chicken's head until each chicken went to sleep. The chickens were as obedient as well trained babies. We lived in an unpainted, frame, two room house with no porch, and a tin roof. Our house was weather beaten, and the wood looked grey. The two rooms were separated by a narrow hallway. One room was used for a kitchen, and the other was our bedroom. Mother's and Daddy's bed was on one side of the room; Mona, Lila, and I shared a bed on the opposite side of the room.

My sisters and I were given the opportunity to choose our places in the bed for sleeping. I quickly chose to sleep in the middle. Mona slept on the front, and Lila slept on the back in the bed. I never told them that I chose to sleep in the middle of the bed to insure my safety. I reasoned to myself, that if a ghost or monster should come up from the front, it would get Mona first, and if one came up from the back side of the bed, it would get Lila instead of me.

Memories of those days when we lived on that bottom land with Mother and Daddy are quite vivid. On Saturday nights, Mother would press Mona's, Lila's, and my hair, using pork lard for hair dressing. On Sundays, Mother would tie our hair up to prevent it from getting dusty as we rode to church in an uncovered wagon. Once we arrived at church, Mother would remove our head rags, and we would go into the Methodist church for service.

Daddy would take the whiskey he made to church sometimes. He would remain on the church grounds until he sold all of his whiskey. Then he would go home. Sometimes the preacher was given free whiskey to preach the bootleggers' favorite sermon. The preacher cooperated. The whiskey stimulated the preacher. He would lean back and holler as he preached. The bootleggers enjoyed hearing their favorite sermon. Whenever the church services were high, Mama Lillie used to shout and laugh loudly. The ushers had to hold and fan those who shouted and rejoiced. Mr. Jessup, one of the church members, used to rejoice in a strange way. He would walk up and down the vacant pews in the church. I loved it when there was peace between my parents. I enjoyed hearing them discuss things that were happening around the countryside where we lived. I especially liked to hear the story about a man named Jeb Higgins.

Mr. Jeb was a sort of stocky man who appeared to have been about forty years old. One night as Mr. Jeb walked down a dark road, Daddy and one of his friends hid in a ditch by the side of the road. As Mr. Jeb passed by, Daddy's friend called out with a loud voice, "Jeb, oh Jeb, go preach!" Now Jeb thought he had been called by a divine power. Therefore, he was obedient to the call. He made haste and began preaching. People laughingly told of Mr. Jeb's false calling into the ministry. If he heard the story, it did not stop him. Although Mr. Jeb never became a good preacher, he continued to preach.

Daddy was a tall, dark, handsome man who had a terrible temper sometimes. Mother was a fair, petite, humble woman with long hair. Daddy made a decent living. In addition to farming, he was a bootlegger. Once, my little world was crushed because he was sentenced to serve one month working on the county road for making and selling whisky. On one occasion, Daddy was beaten badly by white policemen because he was bootlegging corn whiskey. We were told that they beat him and beat him that day. As my father lay on the ground, the cops proceeded to further torture and terrify him by jabbing a pointed shovel hard into the ground around his head. He knew that he could have been killed at any given moment. Finally, they released him. Somebody brought him home. If those white cops had chosen to kill Daddy, there would have been no consequences imposed upon them by the law. That happened in Tennessee during "Jim Crow" days, years before the Civil Rights Movement began. During those days, the white man's word was law. For quite some time afterwards, it seemed that more than Daddy's body was beaten. His spirit also seemed broken and crushed.

While Mona and Lila were in school, mother would send me on errands to my aunt's house alone, which was about a mile away. As I traveled that dusty road alone, my constant prayer was, "Lord, please don't let me see no snake." The Lord honored my prayer. I saw a number of snakes when I was accompanied by someone else, but I never saw a snake when I traveled alone.

Mommy Christy, my paternal grandmother was a kind caring woman. Her mother, Doreen, and father, Jasper, had been slaves. Grandpa Jasper was the son of his old master. Of course he was not mentioned in his father's will. However, the old master did sell Grandpa Jasper 400 acres of land for $1 per acre. The old master had a new home built. He gave the old plantation house to Grandpa Jasper. Mommy Christy and her siblings were raised up in that house.

Mommy Christy died shortly after my sixth birthday. I still had not enrolled in school. During the day, Mother and I were the only people in the bottom except those who were working far away in the fields. I've often wondered if that was the reason mother kept me home with her for so long, instead of sending me to school. My mother's teenage cousin, Flossie Bell, used to visit mother and talk about her extremely jealous husband, Evan. I played around on the floor and pretended that I was not paying attention to their conversation. One day Flossie Bell said, "Cousin Ludie, he even accused me of going with Timothy Lee." I knew that she was innocent.

The next time I saw Flossie Bell at my house was on my sixth birthday. Mother was giving me a birthday party. I will never forget that day. You see, it was on that day I learned that I was capable of being a mischievous liar. I waited until I was alone with Flossie Bell and her husband. Then I said "Floss Bell, where is that letter you wrote Timothy Lee?" I did not notice the expression on Evan's face because my eyes were fixed on Flossie Bell's facial expression of both shock and anger.

She replied, "I didn't write Timothy Lee no letter!" I knew she was telling the truth. But her husband would not have believed a six-year-old child would have made up a lie like that. Mother learned of what I had done. For the first and only time, Mother whipped me on my birthday. Being embarrassed about the whipping, I left the party and hid in a nearby cotton field for a while. Years later I learned that Flossie Bell's husband had beaten her after he got her home. I felt compassion for her after hearing of her beating about my father's younger brother, Timothy Lee. I wanted to tell her I was sorry. But by that time, years had passed, and I did not see her anymore.

A number of things happened during my sixth year which caused me to remember that year vividly. I finally started school that fall. My cousin, Alvin, who was a few months younger than I, was already a grade ahead of me. That did not make me happy. Blairs Elementary was a two room wood frame school house that went through eighth grade. Some of those students looked old enough to have been my parents. Daddy's brother Lonnie, who was sort of a ladies' man, was either dating or had dated several of the teenage girls at school. As a favor to Lonnie, those girls looked after my sisters and me.

In October, my youngest sister, Helena, was born. We had been sent away while the midwife was delivering the baby. When we returned, Mother said, "Perseverance, I have something that looks just like you."

I said, "What is it, a doll?" I walked over to Mother's bed and looked at the little bundle of joy in her arms.

Aunt Estelle (Mother's sister) and her husband, Shelly, had brought Uncle Tommie (Mother's terminally ill brother) to see the baby. Uncle Tommie was a brown skin, small frame man of medium height. He walked through the yard and to our door wearing overalls, a shirt, and a cap. He was crying as he walked. I guess he knew that was the last time he would see Mother and her little family. Mother's brother and sister lived in the city. Uncle Tommie died two weeks later.

When Christmas came that year, my three-year-old cousin, Sylvia, and I were at the home of my maternal grandparents, Lillie and Zack Winston. Mama Lillie was a dark complexion woman of medium height. She had big hips, big legs, and blue eyes. She had no problem with speaking her mind to people who irritated her. Mama Lillie's parents were Betty and Sam Reid. They were former slaves. Grandma Betty was the daughter of her old master. She was 12 years old when slavery ended. She said that she worked in the fields sometimes with her nakedness showing because her clothes were ragged.

Christmas day at my grandparents home was not a happy one for me. Sylvia's parents had bought her a car that was large enough for her to ride in, and other toys. My Christmas presents consisted of fruit, nuts, candy and fifty cents that Papa Zack gave me. Everything was in a shoe box except the fifty cents. Papa Zack was a kind, sensitive man.

Each time visitors dropped in that Christmas day, Mama Lillie would tell them what Sylvia and I got for Christmas. She'd say "Sylvia got a car, doll, etc. Perseverance got some fruit, candy and nuts. Zack gave her fifty cents. Each time she told visitors that, I felt so small and forsaken. Finally, Papa Zack said "Lillie, why don't you hush? You'll make the child feel bad." I was relieved.

In March, while I was yet 6 years old, I spent a few days at Mama Lillie's and Papa Zack's home again. One evening, Papa Zack did not come home from the field. We waited for him until late that night. He still did not come home. That was not characteristic of Papa. Mama Lillie sent Mr. Thompson, a friend of theirs, and Sam, a young man who helped Mama and Papa on the farm, out to search for Papa. When they returned, I knew something was wrong. I looked at Mama, who was already frantic. Mr. Thompson and Sam stood near the door. Mr. Thompson's eyes had gotten wider. The small light complexion man looked scared as he said to Mama, "We found him in the woods, and he's dead." Mama lost it then. She started screaming. They took Mama to a neighbor's home about a quarter of a mile away. My three-year-old cousin Sylvia and I followed the grown ups down the road that night. Sylvia was hollering, "Oh me, Jesus!" After Papa Zack's funeral, Mama Lillie moved to the city in Warrington to live with Aunt Estelle and Uncle Shelly.

After I returned home, I became more aware of Mother's and Daddy's relationship. There were times when Daddy was in a good mood. He'd come home, pick Mother up, set her on his lap and kiss her. At other times, he was quite the opposite. Once I saw him standing over her with a chair raised, daring her to say anything. Mother just sat there looking so humble and fragile as the tears trickled down her cheeks, past her eye glasses, and onto her lap. As I looked on, I didn't know what to do. So I cried too.

Mother never knew what might set him off. On one occasion, when they returned home, Daddy walked ahead of Mother, as he often did. He picked up a pitch fork and began to jab it at her if she tried to enter the door. Mother just stood there quietly until he decided to allow her to enter the house. There were many similar incidents. Sometimes Mother would leave him and take my sisters and me with her to Aunt Estelle's house. Daddy would come to get us, crying and begging Mother to come back home. She would always go back to him. That made me happy because there was security in living with both my parents in our own home.

During those years as a very young child living in that two room house on bottom land in Tennessee with both my parents, I felt more secure than at any other time during my childhood. There were times, however, when that security was threatened. Sometimes when Mother and Daddy were gone away from home, Mona, Lila, and I were alone except for two grown up male relatives who were suppose to have been looking after us. Our parents had no idea that once they left us, those grown up relatives whom I shall refer to as Hawk and Nolan would try to sexually abuse Mother's and Daddy's little girls. They would chase us as we ran as fast as we could. Sometimes Hawk's penis would be exposed. Mona, Lila, and I ran as if our very lives depended on our escaping them. If either of us was ever caught, I must have blocked it out because I have no memory of our having been caught by Nolan or Hawk.

As frightened as my sisters and I were of those incidents, we never told Mother or Daddy. If we had informed Daddy about what was happening, he probably would have lost it. Thus, there might have been tragic consequences. Although Mona, Lila, and I discussed the situation over the years, we never told Mother nor did we discuss the issue with others. I do not remember how old I was when the incidents began. I only know that it happened sometime between my self awareness and age 8. You see, we moved from that bottom land in Tennessee, shortly after my eighth birthday.

Thus, that particular terror ended when we moved into the city. Through that experience, I learned that children don't always tell their parents everything and that as a parent, one should observe and encourage children to share any problems with their parents or guardians. Although trust is important, remember that no one should be exempt from observation until he/she has proven himself/herself to be trustworthy. I have learned to observe when others think I am not paying attention. That may cause those who have child abuse tendencies to let their guard down. Mona did not want me to reveal this secret. She thought it might make a difference in relationships within the family. My response to Mona was, "If we could live through that ordeal, the rest of the family ought to be able to read about it."

After we moved into the city in Warrington, Mona, Lila, and I did not have to worry about being chased by male relatives anymore. A few years later, I learned to be leery and observant of the actions of a family friend named Jonathan. He used to come to visit my mother and grandmother sometime. Although he never bothered my sisters or me, I did not trust him. I had heard the adults in the family discuss the terrible deed he had done. Mr. Jonathan was married to a very nice woman named Mary. They had three children. They lived on the other side of town in Warrington. When his daughter, Susan, was about 12 years old, he raped her one day when they were home alone. We were told that Mr. Jonathan gave her a dime and threatened to kill Susan if she told anyone. However, people did hear about his dastardly deed. Poor little Susan became pregnant with her father's child while she was still a young child herself. I never saw Susan again, but I have often wondered how her life, and the life of her child turned out. I hope that somehow she has been blessed to find happiness. The last time I saw Mr. Jonathan was during the family hour of a deceased relative. More than 25 years had passed then. Nevertheless, I pretended that I did not recognize him because I did not want to speak to him as we greeted other relatives and friends. My actions toward Mr. Jonathan surprised me. It is not characteristic of me to avoid speaking to people.

 CHAPTER 2

CHAPTER 2

When I was seven years old, Daddy got a job working at a plant in Midland, Tennessee. Mother, along with the kids, worked the farm. Mona stayed home to baby sit my youngest sister, Helena. Lila and I helped Mother in the field. Someone made me a little cotton sack to use as I picked cotton. With Mother and Daddy working, they were able to save and buy a car. None of us could have known that Daddy's new job and a new car marked the beginning of the end for us as a family. You see, that's when Karmen came on the scene. She was a young woman who rode to work with Daddy daily. They began to have an affair. Sometimes when they wanted to be together at night, Karmen would drive down the road from our house and blow the horn. Daddy would leave immediately and go to her. Once when Mother confronted him about his affair with the woman, he promised Mother that he would end the affair. Daddy said to Mother, "If I go with Karmen anymore, God is a possum." However, the affair did not end. Things got worse. And the "other woman" became more bold. Everybody around the country side knew about the affair. Once Karmen asked Mother's cousin, Flossie, "Will Ludie fight?"

Flossie Bell answered, "Cousin Ludie is easy going. She said when the Lord gets tired of the way you and Harvey are carrying on, he'll stop it."

Karmen said to Flossie, "Well, I guess she's right, but God o'mighty, when that'll be." During the spring, shortly after my eighth birthday, life, as we had known it, changed forever. Mother had a bad digestive system and was lying down, not feeling well one evening. Daddy came in , looked at her, and got angry. He said to Mother, "Go home and lay up on your folks." Mother got up and packed our little earthly possessions in pillow cases. Late that evening, Mother, my three sisters, and I left our home forever. We walked across the creek. Then we traveled up a hill, and through a field, carrying our pillow cases on our backs until we came to the road that led to Mother's cousin, Flossie Bell's house. Flossie Bell and her husband had a telephone. There, Mother called Aunt Estelle and told her what had happened. I noticed that Flossie Bell was trying to make some kind of cola pop. We didn't have to wait long before Aunt Estelle and Uncle Shelly came to get us. They took Mother and her four children to live with them in the city, in their two room flat. Shortly afterward, Aunt Estelle and Uncle Shelly bought two homes. There was a large home and a two room house on the lot. They allowed us to live in the two room house behind the big house where they lived. Soon after that, Daddy came and asked Mother to take him back. Mother agreed to do so, but she refused to return to the farm with him. So Daddy moved in with us. Unfortunately, that living arrangement put him real close to Karmen's home in the city. Mother and Daddy were living together again, but their relationship was not good. By that time, Karmen had become pregnant. Even though she and her husband were living together, it was no secret that Daddy was the father of her unborn child. During that summer, Karmen's husband was drowned.

Although my parents' relationship was not good, Daddy showed care for us. I remember when I was very young before we moved from the farm, Daddy's younger brother, Timothy, hit me while riding his bike. It was an accident, but my father became very angry with Timothy. My head was bleeding, but I was not badly hurt. Daddy picked me up and carried me in his arms to the house. He walked with his head held high, cursing every step of the way. He never whipped me until I was eight years old. The circumstances surrounding that whipping, are embedded within my memory bank. One Sunday, during the summer that Daddy came to live with us in the city, Mother and the rest of the family went to revival services at the Methodist church of which Mother was a member. The church was in the rural area of Warrington. After service, various families would always spread a big dinner on the tables in the shaded area of the large church ground. So Mother was gone all day. Lila and I were left at home with Daddy. Lila had just turned ten. I was two years younger than she. Daddy decided to go some place that day. My sister and I were left at home alone. We were not afraid though. When Mother came home, she asked us about Daddy. We told her that he went down the railroad tracks and pointed in the direction he went. It never occurred to us that Karmen lived in that direction. When Daddy came home, Mother asked him about it. I guess he thought we were informing on him. He gave me a whipping that made up for all the years before. Then he beat Lila even more. Her beating just continued on and on. Mother tried to say something, but it was as if she was whispering in the wind. I don't remember if the object he was whipping Lila with broke or not. I do know that as others stood around on the porch and in our yard, Daddy walked several feet away, picked up a plank of wood, and started back towards Lila. He was not finished beating her yet. As he came toward her with the plank of wood, my sister tried to hide behind somebody. By that time, Lila was not crying anymore. The noises that came from her sounded like coarse, frantic groans. It was Aunt Estelle who stepped in and threatened him. Daddy put the plank of wood down and left Lila alone. My aunt was not easy going like Mother was. She carried an ice pick in her bosom. Therefore, Daddy knew that her threat was sincere. That was the last summer he spent with us. What happened that evening has caused me to wonder if my parents' broken marriage was a blessing in disguise for us.

I started second grade in the city that fall. My teacher was a mean lady who looked to have been about forty years old. Her name was Mrs. Lovette. In her mean "no nonsense" voice, Mrs. Lovette said to the class "There will be no printing in this class.

Everyone must write in cursive." I knew nothing about writing in cursive, but I was afraid to tell her so. Therefore, I just printed and drew a line from one letter to the other, hooking them together. I never knew what Mrs. Lovette thought about my writing.

During that fall, Karmen gave birth to Daddy's child. Daddy's brother, Lonnie, lived with us also. He told Mother that Karmen was going to give Daddy a wrist watch for a Christmas present. Sure enough, he got into bed with Mother one night, wearing his new wrist watch. When Mother told him he could not sleep with her wearing that watch, he got up and went to live with Karmen. So he left Mother and four little girls behind. I was eight years old, Helena was two, Lila was ten, and Mona was eleven. Mother was hurt, but she didn't let anyone see her cry. Sometimes, late at night, when she thought everyone else was asleep, she would cry. You see, I was not always asleep. But I never let her know I was awake.

During that winter, one positive thing happened for me. I was assigned to a nice teacher's room when I passed to 2A, the second half of the second grade. Unlike many of the other teachers who seemed to favor little light complexion girls with long hair or students from the homes of educated parents, Mrs. Suttlers favored me, a little poverty stricken girl. She was a kind Christian lady who looked to have been about thirty years old. I shall never forget that lady. She made me her little helper. She would send me on errands. Only the chosen few students were sent to a nearby high school to buy their teachers' lunches. Mrs. Suttlers chose me. Her attitude of confidence in me caused my intellect to surface. My self esteem was raised. I became more aware of my manners and my speech. Some of the other teachers noticed and commented on my politeness and the way I conducted myself when I entered their rooms. Finally, spring came. Mrs. Suttlers chose me to play one of the little fairies in the school play. New clothes were not easy to come by, but Mother bought me a beautiful white dress to wear in the school play. Near the end of the school year, students at South Warrington Elementary, the school that I attended, had an opportunity to go on a trip to the Memphis Zoo. The cost was $1.10. Unfortunately, Mother did not have the money to pay my fare. One day, just before the trip, Mrs. Suttlers asked me to stay after class was over that evening. She always called me by my middle name. She said, "Louise, run home and ask your mother if she will pack a lunch for you if I pay your fare to go to the zoo in Memphis." So I ran home and excitedly told Mother what my teacher had said. Mama Lillie, my grandmother, listened as I told Mother. It was Mama Lillie who unpinned her little tobacco sack from her bosom, and gave me $1.10 from it. I ran back to school that evening and gave the money to my teacher. So, I went on the trip to the Memphis Zoo. School was almost out, and I had just turned nine years old.

Daddy never came back to live with us again. Sometimes Karmen would push the buggy that carried hers and Daddy's baby past our house. Mother saw her but never said anything. Later that year, Daddy and Karmen moved to Chicago. Their moving away was better for Mother. Once I heard Mother tell someone that she was crying on the inside. Shortly after that, Daddy and Karmen had a second child.

At nine years old, I entered the third grade. That was not a good year for me. My new teacher was a big robust, mean, and insensitive woman named Mrs. Greer. She would make us lie across a chair, and pull our dresses tightly while she beat us with a paddle about ½ inch thick and 3 inches wide. She would send students to Savage's Restaurant, just behind the school, to get double dips of ice cream and chewing gum. She would eat the ice cream in the classroom. It must have been delicious because as she ate it, she would say, "I could just go out and shut the door." She would also chew gum as if it was candy. As we looked on, we dared not say anything to make her angry, or it would have been the "chair and paddle" for us.

One day, as Mrs. Greer walked around in class, she said loudly, "Someone has a strong under arm odor, and it's you!" She was pointing to me. I felt so humiliated. She also told another girl in class that her coat needed a bath. I felt small and insignificant. The pride and confidence that I felt the year before had vanished. My self-esteem was almost floor level. That winter, I had whooping cough. It was not a mild case for me. My cough was terrible, and the white of my eyes was as red as blood. Mother was worried about me. Someone told her about a particular kind of tea to brew for me. Mother made the tea for me. Sure enough, my condition improved rapidly. She told me that the tea was made from some kind of herb in our front yard. It tasted like coffee. When I was well, I asked her to show me the herb in the yard. She never did. I later learned that the tea I drank was made from cow manure. Whenever Mother would bring my food into the bedroom for me to eat, Helena would crawl up in the bed with me and hide where Mother couldn't see her, and help me eat my food. At the time I was too weak to eat very much, so whatever I didn't eat, she would. I later came down with measles. When I recovered from that, I returned to school and the mean, insensitive teacher. Upon my return, Mrs. Greer quickly informed me that I was going to fail the third grade. I didn't say anything then because I didn't want her to embarrass me in the presence of the class. Later, I called her at her home and pleaded with her to pass me. She knew I had been ill. I was a smart little girl, and I would have worked very hard to make up for the time I was out. I was not surprised when she replied with a definite "No" to my plea. That teacher had a negative impact on my life. It took me a few years to get over her embarrassing me in the classroom and my failing the third grade.

After Mother learned that I was not going to pass anyway, she did not send me back to school for the rest of that school year. We lived with my grandmother and Mother's youngest brother, Curtis. Uncle Curtis worked for a tire company down town, or "up town" as we called it. Mother worked as a cleaning lady in a white beauty shop. My grandmother took care of us while Mother worked. Since I was not going to school, my grandmother gave me the job of taking Uncle Curtis a hot lunch daily. I used to wear a straw hat after the weather got warm, and one of the two dresses that Mother made for me from flour sacks. One was white with red polka dots, and the other was white with green polka dots. Sometimes I walked bare feet. The concrete would be so hot, it would burn my bare feet. I would raise one foot and shake it. Then I raised the other foot from the concrete to shake for coolness. One day, as I was on my way to take Uncle Curtis his lunch, Whimpy, a little, white, shaggy, meddlesome dog who lived a few houses up the street from us, ran out into the street barking as if he was going to attack me. As I was fighting Whimpy off with Uncle Curtis' lunch box, Mr. Sonny Boy, Whimpy's owner, came out to call the dog off me. By that time, Uncle Curtis' lunch was out on the street. I didn't dare go back home to tell my grandmother that the lunch she had prepared for her son was ruined. That would have caused me to get a good whipping. Therefore, I scooped up the lunch which consisted of cornbread, black eyed peas and pork chops, from the street, placed it in the lunch box carefully, and took the lunch to Uncle Curtis. He ate as if he enjoyed it. If the food tasted gritty after having been on the concrete, Uncle Curtis probably attributed it to Mama Lillie's cooking.

I remember that I never tasted barbeque as delicious as Uncle Kurt's was. When we lived in that little two room house on South Street in Warrington, my uncle used to barbeque whole hogs. He would dig a space in the back yard that was long and wide enough to be used as an open pit for a whole hog, except for its head, feet and insides. After the fire had cleared, a large rack was placed over the smoking pit. The cleaned hog was placed on the rack. Uncle Kurt used to sit up most of the night barbecuing. In the morning, there was plenty for us to eat. He also sold a lot of barbecue with his special sauce. One Saturday morning I listened as a new customer explained how he heard of Uncle Kurt's barbecue. The small framed, dark complexioned man spoke with an accent that was alien to my ears. The man talked in run-on sentences as he said to my uncle, "I was sitting at the table this morning, drinking meself a coffee, and whatchamacallit says to me, 'Fellow, barbecue!' I says 'Where?' He says, 'Down on the low end of Institute Street.' I got right up from the table, quit drinking meself a coffee, and came on down here." After listening to that customer talk, I rolled around on the bedroom floor laughing.

One night Daddy called Mother from Chicago. I was happy to hear his voice when I answered the telephone. When Mother got off the phone, she told us that Daddy wanted her to come to him in Chicago. Although he had a woman and two children, I was very excited because Mother was still his wife and there could have been a chance for us as a family. I jumped and shouted, yelling, "Mother and Daddy are getting back together. Mother and Daddy are getting back together!" Daddy and Karmen had separated. She had returned to Warrington. Mother borrowed money from Aunt Ida, my grandmother's sister, to buy the things she needed for the trip. I can still visualize the long red coat she bought. Other people were happy for Mother and us. Shortly before time for Mother to leave for Chicago, Daddy called and told her to not come to Chicago. We were hurt and disappointed. It wasn't long before we learned that Karmen had gone back to Daddy in Chicago. People in our hometown did not know that Daddy had told Mother he didn't want her to come to him. They assumed that Karmen had heard that Mother was going to Daddy and decided that she was going to get there first. That rumor enabled Mother to salvage a little pride.

Our financial situation became more difficult at home because Mother had to pay back the money she borrowed when getting prepared for her move to Chicago. She only earned seven dollars per week. Mother had filed for child support, but Daddy fought it. That was the beginning of my sisters and me growing up on one meal per day. We had no breakfast or lunch. When we came home from school in the evening, my grandmother would have pinto beans and corn bread, which was cooked on top of the stove, ready for us to eat. Once Mona complained to one of Daddy's younger brothers that we weren't getting much financial help from Daddy. Our uncle replied hatefully, "He didn't have to send you nothing!" Over the years, I have observed that uncle as he exemplified the characteristics of a wonderful father to his children, even after they grew up.

Somehow, Karmen had gotten the address of the beauty shop where Mother worked as a cleaning lady. She wrote Mother a letter telling her off. She read the letter while at work, as the white women for whom she worked looked on. The women giggled and asked, "Ludie, is your husband saying sweet things to you?" I watched Mother read it again after she came home. I do not remember the entire contents of the two letters. However, some of those words shall be embedded within my memory bank until the day I die. Karmen said to Mother in her letter, "If he had wanted you, he would have stayed with you. Anyway, I wouldn't want a husband who had children by another woman!" As a means of proving to Mother that Daddy really did not want her, Karmen enclosed a letter that Daddy had written her after she left him in Chicago. She knew that Mother would recognize Daddy's handwriting. Daddy said in his letter to Karmen, "I love you, and I can't give you up." As Mother read both letters, the pages fell to the floor, one at a time, as if they had a sense of direction of their own, and the tears streamed down her face. I felt so sorry for Mother. I gave her a towel to wipe away her tears. She hugged me tightly, as her frail body seemed to shake almost beyond endurance.

Sometime later, Mother did some house cleaning for one of her employer's at the beauty shop. While at the employer's home, the employer's mother-in-law informed Mother that the women for whom she worked, had already read the letters that Karmen sent before they gave the mail to Mother. Since they already knew the contents of those letters, how could they have giggled and made sport of Mother's misery?

After writing the above passage this morning, I paused and wept for Mother who has been deceased now for nine months. It was my daughter, Shawny, who reminded me that Mother is in a better place now. She's happy with Jesus. I knew she was right. Yesterday, I had to comfort Shawny. It was she who cried and cried after learning the content of my writing. We're all right now.

I shall resume my story. During the late 1940s Aunt Estelle and Uncle Shelly moved to Detroit. They allowed us to live in the big house. It had five rooms and an inside bathroom. The house had a living room, two bedrooms, a small breakfast nook, and a tiny kitchen. There was also a long hallway. The house was already furnished. Aunt Estelle and Uncle Shelly took nothing to Detroit with them except their clothing. I don't know what we would have done had it not been for my uncle and aunt. Daddy's brother, Lonnie also offered to help Mother with us. I wish I could let them all know how very grateful I am for the help they gave us. But they are all gone now. They can't hear me say, "Thank you."

Not long after Aunt Estelle and Uncle Shelly moved away, Daddy and Karmen decided to come back to Warrington to live. After Mother learned that they had made Warrington their home again, she got down on her knees and began to pray. I heard Mother say, "Lord, I can't live in the same city with them anymore." The Lord answered her prayer. Daddy and Karmen went back to Chicago and never came back to Warrington to live again.

 **CHAPTER 3**

CHAPTER 3

Mother finally accepted the fact that all hope was gone for hers and Daddy's marriage. She divorced him, and Daddy married Karmen. Mother got a job working in a produce house. There she met the man who became my stepfather. His name was Sam Jones. He was tall and dark with sort of a hefty medium build. He appeared to have been several years Mother's senior. My sisters and I always called him Mr. Sam. Mr. Sam lived in a four room house about a mile down the railroad from where we lived with my grandmother and my uncle. So, Mother was finally able to move into a home that she could call her own. Mr. Sam had a lot of junk in his house, and several black cats. Mother cleaned the house, got rid of the junk, and bought new furniture, but she did not get rid of those black cats. One cat had a lot of missing hair from its body. You could see bare skin. One evening Mother cooked steak for dinner. I could not enjoy the steak, for thinking about the cat with the missing fur. I'm not a lover of steak today because it reminds me of that bare skin black cat. My stepfather seemed proud to show off his new bride. I understood why. Mother was a nice, good looking woman. His attitude toward my sisters and me was indifferent. He wasn't the best or worst stepfather. We all cared about him, simply because he was there. I guess he didn't want Mother to spend money on us because once when she bought me a skirt, blouse, and a pair of shoes, she told me to hide them so that he wouldn't see them.

When I was ten years old, I resolved that it was time for me to prepare myself for a relationship with the Lord. Mother was a member of a Methodist church out in the country. It was inconvenient for me to attend Mother's church often. So I started attending a Baptist church in town. During revival, I placed myself on the mourners bench with a number of other children. That was the front bench in church, where various grown ups worked with us as we tried to get religion. Today, we refer to the same situation as "seeking salvation at the altar." The Baptist church which I attended was about twelve blocks from my home. Since my feet were my favorite source of transportation, I did not mind the long walk. I always got my clothing and myself ready for church. However, I was never good at doing my hair. So Mother would have Mona or Lila do my hair. I never had a problem with Mona doing my hair; but Lila used to burn my scalp and laugh about it as I cried. I attended church each Sunday. While walking to church, I had to pass Mr. Moody's house. Mr. Moody was an elderly white man who Mother borrowed money from. Sometimes when we were in dire need of money, Mother would write a note to Mr. Moody, asking to borrow five or ten dollars. We would take the note to his house. Mr Moody always sent the money. Of course Mother had to repay the money with interest. Nevertheless, the old white man's willingness to lend was beneficial to our family. Mr. Moody was neither mean, nor friendly. Yet as I passed his house each Sunday, as I walked to church, I remembered that the person who lived there represented financial help for my family.

One night while at church, I felt that I had gotten religion. I shouted around, and later joined the Baptist church, and was baptized. I attended church faithfully and paid close attention to the preacher's sermon. Mother would ask me to tell her about the preacher's message each Sunday when I got home. That made me feel good because Mother would praise me for being able to explain in depth, the preacher's sermon. I also began to read the Bible a lot at night. Even though I read silently, it must have aggravated Lila because as I read one night, she got out of bed, and turned the lights off.

One Sunday, Lila said she was going to church with me. So

my sister and I embarked upon our journey to church. Before arriving at church, Lila talked me into going to visit a girlfriend of hers instead. Lila's friend lived more than two miles away. When the visit was over, Lila and I returned home as if we were coming from church. Mother asked me to tell her about the preacher's sermon. My discussion about the sermon was a complete lie. However, I thought I lied well. Unfortunately, Mrs. Jacobs, who lived down the street, had already told Mother that she did not see Lila and me at church. Since our neighbor was an adult, her word was law. So, Mother whipped Lila and me.

One summer, when Daddy and Karmen came back to Warrington on vacation, he came to my grandmother's home to visit us. When he left, I walked him part of the way back to where he and Karmen were staying. During the walk, he casually asked about Mother. He didn't show any real interest. Later, I headed down the railroad track to Mother's house. When I got there, I told another big lie. I told Mother that as I walked with Daddy, he questioned me about her and where she lived. I also told her that he stopped on the railroad track and looked longingly towards the home in which she lived. For sometime after that, Mother would call me into the room where she was, and ask me to tell her again what Daddy said and how he acted. I always told the same straight lie. I told her what I knew she wanted to hear and what I wished was true.

I repeated the third grade with that mean, insensitive woman as a teacher. When I saw Mrs. Suttlers, my second grade teacher, she looked at me pityingly, and said, "I wouldn't have failed you." The only enjoyable thing that happened that school year was on Halloween. The school had a Halloween party. There was a contest. The person who looked worst would win first prize. My sister, Lila, and I competed in the contest. We had no costumes. Therefore, we dressed ourselves in old clothing and made our faces up. Lila looked terrible, but neither she, nor the other students looked as horrible as I did. Lila must have known that because she made me stand behind her when they were judging. She was taller than I. The judges chose Lila for first prize. However, her little glory was short lived. When she stepped out to accept first prize, the judges saw me! Then the first prize was given to me. I went through the rest of the school year in sort of a daze. I was no trouble to anyone. Neither was I interested in getting close to any of my classmates. I did my assignments because I did not want to fail again. Finally that school year was over.

My fourth grade teacher was nice, but firm. She was a middle aged lady named Ms. Olden. Sometimes, when she would get tired of a student named Geraldine snitching on other students, she would call Geraldine up to her desk and whip her hands with a paddle. There were other times when students aggravated her by constantly asking her the meaning of various words as we read silently. Finally, Ms. Olden would say, "When you get to a big word, just say elephant, and keep going."

I began to take an interest in school and classmates again. I was fortunate to get a nice teacher for fifth grade. She was a slim, young, attractive lady named Ms. Reed. She appreciated me as a good student. My self esteem began to surface again. I had a little group of nice friends. Only one thing kept me from being completely happy during that school year. There was this big girl named Paulette, who constantly picked on me. She was two grades higher than I. She was already dating. In those days, there were quite a few older girls in low grades. Sometimes as I passed by Paulette, she would say to me, "I can't stand you. You think you're cute." There were other times when she'd say, "I'm going to get you after school!" I was not afraid of students who were my own size. I had lots of fights, but I never started one. That big girl frightened me. I could not understand why she wanted to pick on a little girl like me.

One day, one of Paulette's friends, Thea, who was bigger than Paulette, took my current event paper and refused to give it back to me. I must have snapped because everybody said I hit that big girl first. I only remember fighting like mad. I never passed the first lick before. I didn't believe in tap licks. Once a fight started,

I gave my opponent all that I had to give. I never had to fight the same person twice. When the fight with Thea started, I had one of the three ink containers from a ballpoint pen in my right hand. I was not even aware of it. That big girl was beaten down that day. Her teacher said she had never seen anyone get beaten out of her shoes before. I don't know if Thea ever found her shoes. I did not become aware that a part from a ballpoint pen was in my hand until the fight was over. As Paulette's friend and I fought, Paulette looked on. After the fight was over, Paulette said to me "It looked like you were hitting that girl with lead!" I said to myself, "I was."

That fight marked the end of Paulette's picking on me, and threatening to beat me up after school. After that, we became friends. I used to go to her house to visit.

My mother and stepfather had a son. I asked her to name him Curtis. She did so. I guess she thought I wanted him to be named after her brother, Curtis. But I really wanted him to be named after my boyfriend, Curtis. I couldn't tell her that because she would have whipped me. Although Mother had remarried, times were still hard. My stepfather did not hold jobs for very long. He was not a very good provider. Mother worked as a maid for white people. Daddy always remembered us on our birthdays, Christmas and Easter. Once in a while, he'd send fifteen or twenty dollars for the four of us to divide. For Christmas and Easter, Daddy would send sixty or eighty dollars to be divided among us. My mother and stepfather separated for quite some time. When I was eleven years old, it became necessary for my two older sisters and me to chop and pick cotton to help support the family. We also picked strawberries. I hated those times when we had to go to the field while most of our friends went to school. Shortly after sunrise, the white man's big truck would come into town to pick up hired hands for the day. The pay was $2.50-$3.00 for every hundred pounds of cotton a person picked. We worked until late evening. Then we were hauled back home like a herd of cattle on the back of the white boss' truck. When we went through certain areas of town, we would hide so that other kids who did not have to work as hired hands would not see us. I also hated working in the fields because I was afraid of snakes, worms, and spiders. When we chopped cotton, the rows were so long, we could not see the end of them. When we finally did reach the end, we had to begin chopping on another row coming back in the opposite direction. My sister, Lila said it was so hot, she could see monkeys dancing in front of her.

On one occasion, Thanksgiving found us in the cotton field. The middle aged white boss came in the field as we were working. He said to us, with a certain nasal emission, "My wife has a surprise for y'all." Although he didn't say what the surprise was, I began to visualize a turkey sandwich because it was Thanksgiving. I could hardly wait. I remember thinking that I had never had a turkey sandwich before. Soon afterward, my pleasant imagination was erased by disappointment. Our "surprise" was cookies that were almost as hard as bricks. I was poverty stricken and hungry, but I didn't want those cookies. They were unfit for a dog to consume. We did have a surprise, however, when we arrived home that evening. My paternal grandfather had brought us a turkey, and Mother had cooked it for Thanksgiving dinner. Sometime earlier, I had asked Papa Gene to give us a turkey. Mama Lillie did not believe he would give it to us. She offered a $1.00 wager. So we had our turkey, and I collected my $1.00 from Mama Lillie.

We spent a lot of time either working in the fields or in white folks' homes to help supplement the family income. Somehow we always managed to do our school work and pass our classes. Once when Mother worked as a cleaning lady for the Mass family in the suburbs, she took me to work with her. Mr. Mass' next door neighbor, Mr. Jones, asked if I could clean his house for $5.00. Mother allowed me to do so. I went next door and worked hard cleaning Mr. Jones' house. At the end of the day, he gave me some old faded clothes that belonged to his daughter instead of paying me the $5.00. He became angry when I asked for the $5.00 instead. I then went back next door and waited to catch the bus home with Mother. While waiting for Mother to finish her work, Mr. Jones came back over to Mr. Mass' house. He talked about us to Mr. Mass while in our presence. He referred to us as "The Darkies." Neither Mother nor I said anything. We knew it would not have been healthy to do otherwise. Mother's boss was decent enough to remain silent while Mr. Jones ridiculed us. You see, we lived in the south during "Jim Crow" days. The Civil Rights Movement had not yet begun. I rode the back of those buses, entered the back doors of restaurants, stood at a back window to buy ice cream at the dairy queen, and I was among those who had to drink from separate fountains. Although we lived in the same neighborhood as some white people, we did not live on the same street, and most of their homes were nicer than the homes of blacks. We lived separate lives from white folks and stayed out of their way. Thus, we stayed out of trouble.

One night, as my sister, Mona, and I walked down Royal, a street where whites lived, a group of white teenage boys walked behind us. They began to sing loudly, "Get out of my way, one nigger I told!" My sister and I scurried out of their way. They passed by and left us alone. On another occasion, when I was 14 years old, Mona and I walked down Royal Street. We passed a bakery where a group of young white men were gathered in front of the bakery. They seemed to have been employees there. I remember that one of the men said, in reference to me, "She's fine as wine in the summer time!" Another one said to me, "You're too fine to be a nigger." I resented the word "nigger." However, I knew that it would not have been healthy for me to show anger. Therefore, I continued walking and talking to my sister as if I did not hear what the men had said pertaining to me. My action to what was said was a safety mechanism.

 **CHAPTER 4**

CHAPTER 4

During those days, my sister Lila and I began to realize that there was a marked difference made between Mona and us. Mona was definitely the favorite child of all close relatives on my mother's side of the family. If we went someplace and did not get back home by curfew time, we felt sure we would not get a whipping because they would not want to whip Mona. However, once they did surprise us by whipping Lila, Mona and me. Once Mona read or heard that according to the Bible, the devil went into some swines. Therefore, she did not want to sin by eating pork. So, as poverty stricken as we were, my mother and grandmother bought beef for Mona while Lila and I ate fat, salt pork. On those rare occasions when we had ham or some other lean pork, Mona would steal the pork and eat it. Food was cooked on a wood stove which had a top part called "the warmer," where food was kept after it was cooked. I could always tell when Mona was stealing that food because she hissed like a snake, as her hand rose to the warmer to get that lean pork. I always informed the adults of what she was doing. However, they did not believe me. I always felt that parents who favor one child over the other, do that child a disservice when they show favortism towards the child. There is a price to be paid for being the favorite. It makes a difference in the relationship among siblings. It causes jealousy and resentment. Lila used to pick at Mona. I never said mean things to her, but I laughed about things that Lila said. Mona later told me that she would be more angry with me for laughing, than she was with Lila for saying mean things. I loved my oldest sister dearly and looked up to her; but in situations where a difference was made between us, I identified with Lila because we were in the "same boat."

Mona and Lila were my older sisters. Yet each one chose me to accompany her when she went to visit friends, go for walks, and many other places. It was ironic that they never chose each other. Of course I was elated to be a running buddy of both my sisters. Lila was tall, slim and beautiful. She was very outgoing, and too trusting of her many associates. As beautiful as she was, fellows did not show much interest in her. Neither did Lila seem to care about them. Mona was an attractive girl of medium height. She seemed mature for her age. She was very selective in choosing her friends. She was not too trusting of people. Unlike Lila, Mona and I were interested in boys at an early age, and fellows took to us like ducks take to water. Before Mother allowed Mona to date, she'd go for walks in the evening, hoping to see some boy she liked. She always took me along with her. I observed well. When she was allowed to date, I would hang around to keep an eye on her. Then I would make my report to Mother. Once Mona went to the movie with a fellow named James. Mother told me to follow them. She gave me movie fare and said, "Stay close enough to them to see what's going on, but don't let the boy know you're following them." So I followed my sister and her date down the street until I saw my boyfriend. I forgot about my spying job and went to the movie with my boyfriend. I didn't even know which theatre Mona and her boyfriend went to. She got back home before I did. Mother gave me an old fashion whipping. She never told me to spy on Mona again. Through the years, I've kiddingly told Mona that she ruined me. Watching her caused me to acquire an interest in boys at an early age.

In August of that year, Aunt Estelle and Uncle Shelly, who lived in Detroit, came back to Warrington on vacation. I was scheduled to enter 7th grade that fall. I asked permission to go back home with them. Mother agreed for me to accompany Aunt

Estelle home and attend school in Detroit. I bought some ink remover and removed the 7 from my report card and replaced it with an eight. I had never gotten over having failed the third grade. None of the adults knew what I had done. Shortly afterward, we embarked upon our journey to Detroit. Aunt Estelle and Uncle Shelly lived on the far east side. My aunt took me to enroll in a nearby intermediate school. Evidently I didn't do a very good job of removing that seven from my report card and replacing it with an eight. My new counselor saw right through it. She questioned me in depth about it. I insisted that I was in the eighth grade. Since my counselor was so suspicious, I decided to go to her and confess before the day was over. Then she scheduled me into seventh grade. After about a month, Aunt Estelle and Uncle Shelly moved to the near east side of Detroit. I was given a transfer to Greusel Intermediate school. I bought some more ink remover. I removed the seven from my transfer, and replaced it with an eight. I must have done a better job than before because no one at the new school was suspicious. So I went into the eighth grade. I could certainly do the work. I was very happy. My aunt had bought nice school clothes for me. I had made lots of friends and had become a popular little girl. I had no idea that my joy bubble would explode. Two months later, I was called into the main office by my eighth grade counselor. My records had arrived from the previous school. My counselor was angry because I lied about my grade. Once again, I was put back into the seventh grade. I felt so humiliated.

It was about a month before Christmas. I went through the motion of going to school everyday and doing my work. However, I was no longer interested in the school that I had loved so much. Neither was I interested in living in Detroit anymore. I told Aunt Estelle that I wanted to go back to Tennessee for Christmas. She was unhappy but consented for me to do so. Greusel School gave me a transfer to Tennessee. A few days before Christmas, my aunt put me on a train bound for Tennessee. I had to change over in Chicago. I was so happy to be back in Warrington again. My little eight year old sister, Helena, had gotten chubby. Mona had gotten married at age 17. Her husband had moved into our already crowded home. Finally, the Christmas season was over. It was time to enroll in school in Warrington again. Therefore, I bought me some more ink remover. I removed the seven from my transfer and replaced it with an eight. I had no problem with any staff members. However, the seventh grade students were angry. They told their teacher that I was suppose to be in the seventh grade, not in the eighth. After learning what they had told their teacher, I decided to nip that in the bud. So I went to talk with the seventh grade teacher. I told her that I had been double-promoted while in Detroit because of my age. Finally, the kids stopped trying to make trouble for me. I finished the eighth grade and was never put back again.

During that winter, something else happened that stands out most vividly in my mind. Mona, my newly wed sister, and her husband were going to his parents house for dinner. Mona did not have a decent coat to wear. For the first time, I had a nice, new coat that Aunt Estelle had bought me while I was in Detroit. Mother asked me to let my sister wear my new coat to her in-laws house that evening. I consented for her to wear it because I had no place to go, I thought. I was the running buddy of both my sisters. Lila had a date with a young man named Bob. Her friend Muriel, had a date with his friend, Clay. Although I was not allowed to date yet, Bob had another friend whom he wanted me to meet. His name was Kenny. The only coat I had to wear was a little thin, short corduroy jacket that had no lining. However, I agreed to go with them on that triple date. Bob was the only person with a car. So he picked everybody up. Mother only knew that I was going off with Lila and her friend. She did not know that there was a fellow for me. It was a cold night. Bob's friend Kenny, seemed decent enough. He sure was good looking. They decided to go to a teen hangout in a nearby town. We were then driven to a house in a rural area of that town. The house supposedly belonged to a member of Clay's family. The area was dark, and the house looked deserted. We realized that the intentions of those young men were not honorable. They tried to persuade us to come into the abandoned looking house. We refused. The three boys went on inside and left us in the car. I guess they thought we would come inside if we got cold enough in the car. They were mistaken. After a while, the three of them came outside, near the car wearing white sheets. I guess that was an act to frighten us out of the car. My sister's friend Muriel, said, "Lets go in and let them use protection." Lila said, "Never!" Her response was sharp and angry. The suggestion was not made again. Lila, Muriel and I sat in that cold car all night, while the three young men stayed in the warm house. I was so proud of my big sister for being strong and upholding her moral values.

Early the following morning, they took us back to Warrington. We were put out a few blocks from home. By that time, the boys were angry with us, and afraid of the action our families might take. Nothing like that had ever happened before. Our family and Muriel's family were frantic. Everybody in the community knew everybody. Our families had been inquiring about our whereabouts all night. Therefore, as we three girls walked down the street during late morning, various neighbors stood on their porches and stared at us as if we were low life creatures. We were innocent, but who would have believed us? I was ashamed to be on the outside as we walked down the street. So I walked between Lila and Muriel as if they could hide me from the accusing stares of neighbors. When we arrived home, we explained what happened. Nevertheless, Mother was going to whip us. It was ironic that my grandmother was the one who spoke up on our behalf. You see, Lila and I had never had a good relationship with her. Mama Lillie said, "Sometimes boys will keep girls out if they don't do what they want them to do." As I listened to her, I thought "How perceptive this tough old lady is." Of course Mother didn't whip us because Mama Lillie's word was "law" in that house. That experience taught me that a young lady should never travel into unfamiliar territory with a young man. Neither should she ever go on a date with no money.

Shortly afterwards, I saw one of Daddy's brothers while walking down the street one day. Evidently, he had heard about what happened to us, because when I asked my Uncle Timothy for a quarter, he replied hatefully, "Ask that boy you stayed out all night with!" His response totally baffled me. I did not try to explain that I was innocent. I walked away quietly and I never asked him for money again.

During the spring of that year, my stepfather moved to Detroit and got a job working in the auto industry. Shortly afterwards, Mother followed her husband. So my grandmother, Mona and her husband, Lila and I were left in Warrington. Although Mother sent money to my grandmother to take care of us, Mama Lillie still had us on that one meal per day. It wasn't so bad for Lila because she worked to support herself. Lila was sixteen and a half, and I had just turned fifteen years old. We didn't have a lot to eat. So I drank lots of water. I kept my water in a fruit jar in the refrigerator. Someone continually drank my cold water. It angered me, and I had no idea who was drinking it. One day I put lots of Epsom salt in my jar of water, stirred it and waited to find out who the culprit was. I found out after Mona and her husband, Walter, had left for Detroit. Mona's husband was the person who had been drinking my water. I was told that he had an awfully uncomfortable experience while traveling on the train to Detroit. He was constantly running back and forth to the restroom after having consumed the laxative in my drinking water.

Mama Lillie, Lila and I were the only members of my immediate family left in our home in Warrington. Lila and my grandmother did not get along well at all. I have to admit that their negative relationship could have been attributed mainly to my grandmother's treatment of her. Mona and my little brother were her favorites. Even though I was not a favorite, Mama Lillie could tolerate me more than she could Lila. Once Lila called my grandmother, behind her back, a baldheaded S. O. B. As soon as she said it, she got scared. She realized she had said it before the wrong person, me! As a means of preventing me from informing on her, she told me if I told Mama Lillie what she called her, she would say that I was really the one who called her the S. O. B. Her threat worked. I kept my mouth shut. Although my grandmother probably would have believed that Lila was guilty, she would have taken no chance on allowing the guilty person to go free. Therefore, she would have beaten both of us.

Daddy and Karmen came to Warrington on vacation that summer. Both of them came by to see us one night. Daddy came inside first. We all received him warmly. A little later, Karmen got out of the car and came to the door. Mama Lillie met her at the door and told her that she could not come into her house. Karmen turned around and went back to the car. Sometime later, Karmen said to my sister, Lila, "Your mother is a nice person. But I wouldn't fart in Lillie Winston's mouth if she was out of breath, and I wouldn't spit in her ass if her guts were on fire."

Lila had just turned seventeen. She was dating the cousin of her best friend Cathy. Both Cathy and her cousin, Jim, lived in a nearby town about an hour's drive away. One day as Lila was getting ready to catch the train to nearby Dobbsville to spend the night with her friend, Cathy, Mama Lillie tried to persuade her to stay home. My grandmother did not want my sister to spend the night at the home of Jim's cousin without adult supervision. However, Lila would not listen. Since Mother had moved to Detroit a few months before, Mama Lillie was our guardian in Warrington. As my grandmother pleaded with Lila to stay home, Daddy came by to see us before leaving for Chicago. Mama Lillie was relieved to see him. She solicited his help in talking Lila into staying home. I listened as Daddy tried to persuade Lila to change her mind about spending the night with her boyfriend's cousin in an unsupervised setting. As Daddy talked, Lila never said a word. She just turned and leveled her eyes on him. I knew what that stare meant. Lila's stare let him know that he was a poor role model to talk to her about right and wrong. Daddy must have seen a reflection of his life through Lila's eyes. My father was speechless as he dropped his head and walked away. Lila caught the train to nearby Dobbsville as planned. Soon afterwards, summer was over. Aunt Estelle and Uncle Shelly drove to Warrington to move Mama Lillie, Lila and me to Detroit. So I left my home in Warrington forever.

 **C**HAPTER **5**

CHAPTER 5

We arrived in Detroit, and lived in the house that I had left a little more than eight months before. I enrolled in the same intermediate school. I graduated from that school the following June. We moved to the west side of town. My stepfather was laid off from his job in the auto industry. Times were hard again. Mama Lillie and Lila went back to Warrington to live. Soon afterwards, Lila married at age 17 also, to her best friend's cousin. Lila really disliked living in Detroit. That was one of her reasons for moving back to Tennessee. My grandmother was also hoping to get married to a prestigious, well to do old gentleman. However, that marriage did not happen. There was another older gentleman who was in love with Mama Lillie, and wanted to marry her. She thought a lot of that old man but refused to marry him because he was too poor, and he had five grown children living with him on a farm. Mama Lillie was always looking for someone who could contribute to a better living standard for her. Finally, Mama Lillie moved back to Detroit to live with us. Mona and her husband lived with Mother for years. They paid half of all the bills. During those times, we moved all over town. My little sister, Helena and I went to so many different schools it was surprising that we managed to pass our classes. My stepfather got a job working for a construction company. Our financial situation became better for a short time. Soon he was laid off from work again. We moved again to a place called "Black Bottom." That was a poor area on the east side of Detroit. We lived on Lafayette Street, across from Elmwood

Cemetery. During those days, I experienced hunger that I didn't even experience while living in Tennessee. My stepbrother Gene, from Memphis, had come to Detroit to live with us. One day he found a dime. He and I were so happy. He shared the money with me. I thought of what I could buy with a nickel, that would last a long time. I decided to buy five packs of chocolate kits. They cost one penny a piece. When I was seventeen, and in the eleventh grade, I quit school and got a job working in a restaurant. My salary was $25 per week.

Mother had become a member of the Pentecostal Faith shortly after moving to Detroit. She was C. O. G. I. C. She insisted that I attend church with her regularly. I attended but refused to join because I had no interest in living right. My best friend, Odessa, and I planned to get saved when we became middle age. We never considered that many people don't reach that age. It was at our church that I met the man I married. His name was Phil Sloan. When I met him, I had joined the church but was not saved. My pastor's grandson liked me and had gone on a three day fast, praying for me to be his. He was an attractive, nice young man, but I was not interested in a boyfriend in the Holiness church. Both he and the new member, Phil, played the guitar. Phil came highly recommended by one of the church mothers who had known him for a long time. He was tall, dark, handsome, and then some. I have never known anyone who could play the guitar like Phil. He was a young man, but several years my senior. My mother, aunt and one of the other church members got busy trying to play cupid. However, I still had no interest in dating any member of my church. Phil began to show an interest in me. After much persuasion by my mother and aunt, I decided to date him just to satisfy them. The first time he came to see me, neither he, nor I had much to say to each other. I sat on one end of the sofa, and he sat on the other end. He kept coming back. We began to date regularly that spring. To my surprise, by mid summer, I had fallen deeply in love with Phil. He sure knew how to woo a young lady. He was not at all like other young men I had dated. He opened car doors for me, kissed my hand, etc. He also showered me with gifts. He made me feel special. Thus, he won my heart. He worked for Chrysler Corporation, but was laid off at that time. He used to come from across town every morning to take me to work at the restaurant. I had to open the restaurant early in the morning. Therefore, Phil would stay with me until it was very light outside. When it was time for me to get off work in the evening, he would always be there in his new yellow and green Chrysler New Yorker, to pick me up and take me home. Soon afterwards, I became dissatisfied with my boss. He appeared to have been about forty years old. Sometimes, as I was working in the restaurant, my boss and another man would sit around watching me, and talking about buying me clothes from an expensive clothing store. He also owned the theatre next door to the restaurant. He offered to double my salary if I would come to his apartment above the theatre after I got off work. I refused. After that, he began to complain about my work. Therefore, I quit my job. I knew that it was only a matter of time before he fired me.

Phil returned to work in the auto industry that fall. He proposed to me, and I said "yes." We planned to get married secretly and stay on where we were living separately at the time, until we had saved enough money to get our own place. So on December 25, we were married. I was eighteen years old, and he was twenty nine. If he thought I was not going to tell anyone, he was mistaken. I told my family as soon as I got home on the night of the marriage. I didn't live with Mother for long after that. In less than two months, I discovered that I was pregnant. Therefore, I moved in with him at his sister's and brother-in-law's home. Before leaving, Mother gave me a pep talk on how to get along with people while living in their home. My sister-in-law, Marian and I got along well. She was a few years older than Phil. She was kind and understanding. She did not ride roughshod over me because I lived in her home. For that, I shall always be grateful. The first seven and a half months of my marriage was among the happiest times of my life. On our first Valentines Day together, Phil gave me a large box of candy. He also gave me a small heart shaped box of candy which he referred to as "A token of love for Junior."

During that summer, on one occasion, I had an appointment with my obstetrician, whose office was down town. My husband told me to get his brother, who was visiting here from down South, to take me for my appointment. I decided to ride the bus instead. When I arrived home that evening, Phil was very angry with me. He said he had some reports on me from a reliable source and he wanted a divorce. The first great mistake of my marriage was crying at that time. The more I cried, the meaner the words became that came out of his mouth and fell on my ears, and on my heart. How could he have distrusted me, and believed that some other man would have been interested in a woman who was seven and a half months pregnant? He woke me up in bed the next morning and asked, "Are you going to leave, or do I have to leave?" Since it was his sister's home, I said "I'll leave." However, I did not leave, and he said nothing else about it. After that, he often told me to "get out." I did not have to do anything to make him angry. Since I never knew what kind of mood he would be in, I prayed daily, asking God to not let him be angry with me. That happened over a period of several years. My husband broke my spirit. Thus, he was able to control me. My self esteem sagged, and my intellect suffered. I underwent a personality change. I was no longer talkative and outgoing. I became quiet and withdrawn. During that fall, I gave birth to a son. We named him after his father. He certainly was the apple of my husband's eye. We called Phil Jr. "Beau." Phil's negative treatment of me continued. Once when Little Beau was three months old, I took him to my mother's home to visit for a few hours. Phil left us over there for three days. I was so embarrassed. I did not want my relatives to know that he had dumped us. Therefore, I sneaked out of Mother's house to use a public phone. I called home to ask him to come and pick the baby and me up. I was afraid of his reaction to my phone call. I was relieved when my brother-in-law's mother answered the phone and took the message for him. Sure enough, when he came to pick us up, he said if it wasn't for Mrs. Ruth, his brother-in-law's mother, he would have left us at Mother's home.

During that year, my father died. We didn't know that he was ill. Mother dreamed about him. She never told us what happened in the dream, but she said to Mona, "Call and see about your father." Mona called and found out that he was ill. We still did not know he was very ill. Nevertheless, Mona went to Chicago to visit him. When she arrived there, he was near death. Mona called for Lila, Helena and me to come. So Aunt Estelle and Uncle Shelly drove all of us over to Chicago to see Daddy. Mona also called my grandfather in Tennessee. My grandfather also came to see his son. Daddy asked us about Mother, and said that she could have come to see him. Daddy expressed a desire to go back to Warrington. His brother drove him back to his father's home in Tennessee. My grandfather and stepgrandmother took care of him until he died three weeks later. He was forty-four years old.

During that year, my husband's sister, Joan, came from down South to live with us. When Jr. was thirteen and a half months old, I gave birth to a second son, David. By that time, I desperately wanted my own place but Phil paid no attention to my plea. He wouldn't even promise me a place of my own, even though he knew that my brother-in-law said rude things in my presence, pertaining to me. I guess he was tired of us. We were raising a family while renting one room in their home. When David was a toddler, Joan said that he looked like the man who lived next door to us. Occasionally, it was mentioned by other in-laws who lived in the household. I noticed that a difference was made between my two sons. Once my brother-in-law told David, "I don't talk to you. You look too much like Birney." Birney was the young man who lived next door. One of the in-laws even began to call him Birney. When I complained to my husband, he asked, "Are you guilty?" Except for my children, I felt alone there. Sometimes I would send David to spend a few days at my sister, Lila's house as a means of getting him out of our living environment briefly. When one of my sisters came to visit me, sometimes I would stand in the front window as she was leaving and watch her until she was out of sight. As I watched my sister leaving, I would think "There goes someone who really loves me." I hated living with my in-laws. I felt unloved, disrespected and unworthy. As a means of trying to raise my self-esteem, I took a test to enter training for Practical Nurses. The results of that test came on a day when I was not home. However, my sisters-in-law Marian, Joan and Delia were home. When I arrived, I saw my mail lying on the radiator in the living room. I noticed that the envelop which contained the results of my test had been opened. I was concerned about the test results, and whether or not one of my sisters-in-law had opened my mail, and had read the results before I read them. I hoped that it was my husband who opened my mail. I read the results. I had failed the test. Then the other thing I had a dread of happened. My sister-in law, Joan, voluntarily informed me that it was she who opened my mail. I felt disrespected as my self-esteem and intellect seemed to dwindle. I never told Joan that she was out of line. I knew that my husband had her back. Years later, I was so grateful for having failed that test. At that time, I had only a tenth grade education. If I had become a practical nurse, I would have become complacent in that position. Thus, I would never have pursued a college degree. Therefore, failing that test for practical nursing was a blessing in disguise.

One Saturday Beau, David and I were visiting at my mother's home on March 24. I was seven months pregnant with my third son. During our visit, Beau was hit by a car. He was four years old. His skull was burst in, and pushed back against his brain. That day was like living through a terrible nightmare. I picked him up out of the street, and carried him to my mother's house which was a few feet away. I remember making crying sounds, but on that day, the tears would not come. He was taken to Highland Park General Hospital where surgery was performed on him. He was not expected to live. Lila's husband called my husband. Phil's brother went home and waited by the phone to hear the news that Beau was dead. When my husband came in to the hospital waiting room and sat down while our son was in surgery, I lay my head on his lap. As I lay there with my head on his lap, he never tried to comfort me by putting his arms around me, or his hand on my head or shoulder. He did not touch me. He sat there with both arms folded above my head. It seemed odd to me, and I felt unloved. However, I never mentioned it to him; nor did I discuss my feelings with others. You see, the Lord worked a miracle that day; and that was the only important thing. The telephone call that my brother-in-law waited for never came. As we sat in that hospital waiting room, Mother began to pray and rebuke death in the name of Jesus! After a while, Mother said to me, "Beau is going to be all right." The Lord raised Beau up and blessed him with a sound mind. When I took him to the clinic for a check up, the doctor called other doctors and nurses in to see him. He told them of the condition Beau was in when he was brought into the hospital on that Saturday of the accident. Beau and I agreed long ago, that as long as we live, we will fast on March 24, and give thanks to God for healing him. We do not fast, asking for anything. We just want to thank the Lord for what he has already done. Whenever I look at my eldest son, I see a walking miracle.

CHAPTER 6

Chapter 6

When my third son, Lyle, was born, we were still living in that one room, in the home of my in-laws. Joan helped by sharing her room with Beau. When Lyle was a few weeks old, I got a job working in a plant, making folding doors. My sister, Lila and I worked together. That job enabled me to gain back a little of my self esteem. Marian took care of the children for me. She seemed to have loved Lyle as if he was her own. By that time, Beau was in kindergarten. A few months later, Marian and her husband bought a home and moved away. Some women on my job teased me by saying that I ran my sister-in- law and her husband away from their home. I guess that was the only way they could escape us. My husband had no intention of moving out himself. So Phil and I kept the old flat that his sister and her husband had rented. We lived upstairs in a two family flat. The house was old and ragged, but it was a place of my own. We owned only a used refrigerator and two or three straight back chairs. Marian was kind enough to leave us things needed for use in the kitchen and two bedroom suites. Joan tried to help by giving us green draperies for the living room. Phil brought a used green sofa home for our living room. It was so ragged, one could see the cotton behind the material and the straw behind the cotton. I bought a couch cover for it. My husband also bought a used oriental rug for the living room. So we had the basic necessities for family living. Both Phil and I were working then and I began to feel independent. My youngest sister, Helena, who had dropped out of school, came to baby sit for me.

She was a very kind sensitive person. Unfortunately, her obesity caused her to feel self conscious, and to seek refuge in the privacy of home, rather than continuing in school and dealing with the cruelty of her peers. Even though I was six years older than my sister, she confided in me, and I with her.

When I was three months pregnant with Durand, my fourth son, I walked a block and a half to the bus stop one day. I was going to Highland Park Shopping Center. While waiting for the bus, a car pulled up with three young men in it. They offered me a ride. Since I did not believe in riding with strangers, I said, "No, thank you." To my surprise two of the men got out of the car and started walking toward me. One kept one hand in his tan coat pocket. I was terrified. I started walking away from the bus stop. The dark man said, "Leave her alone, Jay." However, Jay (the tall one) paid no attention. He kept coming toward me. When I started running toward home, he ran after me for about a half block. While running, I looked back to see how close he was behind me. Then I heard a car take off fast and loudly. The other two men must have been leaving him. Jay turned around and ran back in the direction of the car, yelling, "Wait for me!" By the time I got home, the incident had devastated me. I remember the man who lived in the downstairs flat, opened the door for me. I went upstairs and got into bed, hoping to calm my nerves. I told Mae, the lady downstairs, what happened. She told me that her husband wanted to go back looking for those men with his gun. When I told my husband what happened, he replied, "What's for you, you're going to get it." He mentioned as an example, the name of a white lady who was killed down South while participating in the Civil Rights Movement. She was from Detroit. For a long time, I would get nervous whenever I thought about what might have happened if they had gotten me into that car. We lived in that neighborhood for nine more months, but I never went back to that bus stop again.

There was a time in my life when Phil was my knight in shining armor. How I loved that man! My sister, Mona, once said to me,

"I'll bet you would get angry with any man who made a pass at Phil's wife." I replied, "Yes, but how did you know?" Mona answered, "Because you are so wild about him!" Phil held a jewel in the palm of his hand. Unfortunately, he failed to recognize its value. Therefore, he did not feel the necessity to cherish it, and handle with care. The company that I worked for, relocated to another city that year, A few months later, we discovered that Helena was ill. The doctor told Mother that my sister had a heart problem. Mother was very concerned, but Helena would minimize the seriousness of her condition when talking to us. However, she did go on a diet. She lost forty pounds. Unfortunately, the weight loss occurred too late. On April 30, Helena went into cardiac arrest and died. Her death was not expected. She was hospitalized at the time, but seemed to have been doing all right. Mother's deep faith in God kept her strong. I never saw her cry for her youngest daughter, but she did not attend her funeral. I remembered the night that Aunt Estelle telephoned me to give the news that Helena had died. Her words were so guarded, I knew that her news was not good. I immediately thought of Mother. You see, I had had recurring dreams about my mother dying. In the dreams, I would weep and weep. On that night, April 30, 1965 my husband had taken Mother to the hospital to visit Helena. As Aunt Estelle talked, her words fell on my ears and into my memory bank like a permanent stamp. She asked, "Did Phil call you?" I said, "No." At that time, I thought she was going to tell me that Mother was gone. She hesitated a little and said, "Helena passed." I knew I was wide awake, yet it seemed like a nightmare. I experienced a feeling of shock, hurt and restlessness. No one was home with me except three young children. So I sent for Mae, the lady who lived in the downstairs flat. When she didn't come right away, I sent for her again. My thoughts went back to Helena's childhood. I thought of what a kind little girl she was. Some of her little friends took advantage of that kindness, and picked on her. She would not defend herself. She was quite the opposite of Lila and me. We didn't believe in starting fights; but if anyone messed with us, we would go to war in a split second. Lila and I informed Helena that if she did not fight kids back when they hit her, we were going to beat her behind. I guess our little sister thought she had a better chance going up against kids her own size than taking a beating from both Lila and me. So she fought back. She fought when they bothered her and when the other kids did not bother her. We only wanted her to defend herself. We wanted her to be able to differentiate between defending herself and starting fights. However, we never said anything to her about it. Her little peers were aggressive kids. I guess they deserved what Helena was dishing out to them then, because of the way they had mistreated her in the past. Her actions stopped her peers from picking on her, and she was able to grow up in peace.

I was reminded of how Helena used to follow me around when I was with my friends. They called her "my shadow." She was responsible for the last whipping I ever received from my mother. She informed Mother that I had ridden on the back of a motorcycle with a young man who worked at the service station a few doors down the street from our home. I was seventeen years old at the time. That ride was frightening. I had already decided before the whipping that I would never ride on the back of a motorcycle again. I was too old to get whippings. It only made me angry. I guess Mother realized it. She never whipped me again. After that, Helena would embarrass me by asking or telling my friends to ask me how old I was when I got my last whipping. I would be so angry with her. Nevertheless, we were close. I lived at home with her for a few years after Mona and Lila were married and had families of their own. After my in-laws moved away when my son Lyle was an infant, Helena became the baby sitter for my three sons. She adored Lyle. When she became ill, I had Beau, David and Lyle include her in their prayers each night. When she died, Lyle was two and a half years old. On Tuesday, two days before her funeral, Lyle and I were home alone. I was in one room, and Lyle was in another. Suddenly Lyle called me loudly saying, "Mom, here comes Helena. She not sick!" I guess he remembered that he had been praying for her to get well. He did not seem frightened as he told me she was there. However, I sure was frightened. I did not go in the room where he was to see, nor did I insist that she was not there. You see, since he had prayed again and again asking God to make her well, if he saw her, he would have thought she was not ill in the hospital anymore. At age two, if Lyle heard anyone say that she was dead, he would not have understood what that meant. Although I do not like to elaborate on the topic of the unknown, I highly suspect that on that day, Lyle really did see Helena. She loved him so much, and he was too young to have been afraid of her. On Thursday, May 6, 1965, I said good-bye to my baby sister forever. Not long afterwards, Karmen heard that one of Daddy's daughters had died. She called to extend her condolences and to find out which one it was. Karmen said to Mother, "I guess you don't want to hear from me." Mother said "Karmen, if you can make it with the Lord, you can make it with me." That was the last time she and Karmen ever talked to each other. Five weeks after Helena's death, I gave birth to our fourth son, Durand.

As I wrote about Helena's life, I was reminded of her big secret. Mother knew much of her secret. However, there were certain details which Helena never wanted Mother to know. She chose to share the details that were kept from Mother, with Mona, Lila and me. Thus, we honored her wishes, and kept her secret. But now that she and Mother are gone, her secret surfaces in my thoughts from time to time. When Helena was seventeen years old, she met and fell in love with a young man named Laslow. My sister was an eleventh grade, poverty stricken minor from an uneducated family. Laslow, on the other hand, was already in his twenties and was a senior in college. Helena told us of how he wooed her. He wrote a poem for her and proposed marriage. Mona, Lila and I knew that he was too old and experienced for her. Nevertheless, we were happy for her. We thought he was a nice person. We helped Helena scrape up money to purchase a Christmas gift for Laslow. She thought he was giving her an engagement ring for Christmas. Therefore, she wanted to give him something nice. I remember her bringing the gift home. It was a glittering Elgin cigarette lighter. Helena gave the young man his gift and enthusiastically looked forward to receiving her engagement ring. However, Christmas came and passed without Laslow giving my sister a gift. Helena was embarrassed and hurt. After continuously asking about a gift, he finally gave her a cheap looking, little necklace. She was disappointed because she did not get the ring. Nevertheless, that gift of pacification appeased her aggravation, and she salvaged a little pride. She was delighted to show the gift to her family; thus letting us know that her boyfriend did care enough about her to give her some kind of gift for Christmas. Helena and Laslow continued dating, and he still talked about marriage and how many kids he wanted to have with her as his wife. She was happy. Unfortunately, that happiness was short-lived. Her happy dream turned into a horrible nightmare.

During the month of January, Helena discovered that she was pregnant. When she informed Laslow of her pregnancy, that nice acting, smooth talking young man became insensitive and belligerent. Finally, Helena talked to Mother about her situation, and the young man's reaction to the news. When Laslow came to visit my sister again, Mother talked to him about his intentions. Helena said that as she listened to him talk to Mother, he sounded like a man without a conscience. He even lied and told Mother he was already married. My sister further stated that she was so proud of Mother for the firm way she stood up to that scoundrel. Mother, who had always been so kind, and much too tolerant of people's mean spirited behavior, told Laslow that she was going to take legal action against him soon thereafter, and have him put out of school. My sister stood nearby as Mother talked with the young man's mother. Laslow's mother suggested to Mother that she take Helena to see Dr. Jones. Everybody knew that Dr. Jones was known for performing abortions. Therefore, Mother refused, saying, "I don't intend for anything to keep me out of the Kingdom of Heaven." After Mother's conversation with Laslow's mother, he began to try to persuade Helena in private, to get an abortion. However, Helena refused continually, because she had always been taught that the taking of a life is a moral wrong. Nevertheless, her dread of bringing shame on the family, and his attempt to persuade, began to wear her resistance down. Thus, reluctantly, Helena finally agreed to have the abortion. I remember the day that Laslow came to take Helena to Dr. Jones' office. I felt so sorry for her. I knew there was a conflict going on within, that was tearing her apart. After the abortion was over, he brought Helena back home and left. He did not come to see her very often after that. It was obvious that he never really cared about Helena. I'm sure his family was relieved to hear that his problem had been resolved. After all, Helena was a girl from the wrong side of the tracks, and Laslow's family was educated, and his father was a prominent attorney. Helena explained in detail, how she felt that day. She told me that as she and Laslow entered the building where Dr. Jones' office was, she saw an old friend of Aunt Estelle's. He had not seen her since she was a little girl. She hoped that he would not recognize her since she was wearing a scarf on her head. Fortunately, he did not seem to remember her. So she and Laslow crept up the stairs, and into the office of the doctor who assisted in altering the course of her life.

Revealing the above story was one of the most difficult things I've ever done. My sister, Mona, pleaded with me to not reveal this secret which has been so well kept for more than forty years. I understand her love and concern for her sister's reputation. However, if her story helps one young reader who experiences a similar situation, then the sharing of Helena's story will have been worth it. The message I'm trying to convey to my readers is, "follow your conscience." That's what you will have to live with constantly. Doing what you think is right, is far more important than society's opinion of you. Helena told Mother that she had miscarried. She preferred that Mother believed the baby was lost quite by accident. She felt it would have hurt Mother much more if she knew that she had an abortion. During the weeks that followed, Helena became very ill. When Mother took her to see a doctor, it was discovered that the embryo had not yet passed from Helena's body. That caused her to be very ill. For a time, the family did not know if Helena was going to pull through or not. I observed as Mother sat by her daughter's bedside and begged the Lord to spare her life. Meanwhile, Laslow and that quack, Dr. Jones were going scott free. God must have heard Mother's prayers because Helena did recover, and began to pull her life back together again. However, she never recovered from the traumatic experience of consenting to have her baby aborted. She once said that she knew God had forgiven her; but it was difficult for her to forgive herself. Helena said that she would sometimes hear a small child saying, "Mommy." But when she'd look around, there was no one. She stated that the consequences of her actions were something she had to live with. I guess one never really escapes some aspects of the past. Laslow died years later without ever having apologized for what he did to Helena.

All of us were hurt because of Helena's death. But my young brother, Curtis underwent a personality change. You see, he and Helena were at home together for years after Mona, Lila, and I had married and left home. So my little sister and brother were close. My mother and stepfather were separated at the time. Since Curtis was the youngest, and the only boy, Mother and Mama Lillie spoiled him rotten. Therefore, when he became less compassionate and was difficult for Mother to control, my sisters and I attributed the change to his having been spoiled. It was not until much later that I realized his change in attitude could have been due to Helena's death. Curtis began acting indifferent toward his family and closer to non-relatives. He developed an interest in older women. One woman whom he developed a relationship with was old enough to have been his mother. For a few years, it seemed that Curtis was trying to find himself. I thank God that Mother lived to see my brother develop into a caring, dependable, well adjusted young man of whom she could be proud.

The author's great grandparents, Sam and Betty Reid. They were slaves and Betty was the daughter of her old master.

The author in an early school class picture at Blairs elementary.

Doris L. Marshall-Slack

Doris L. Marshall-Slack
1975 Graduation Photos

1975   1979   1984

The author is depicted above in various stages of her educational career.

The Black Studies Club at Murray-Wright High School in 1979. The author is seated in the front row, fourth from the left.

l. to r.-Doris Slack, Beatrice Slack, Tommy, and Shawny Slack on Father's Day 2002

Dave, I already miss you greatly. You were a wonderful son who has shown loyalty to all those you loved. You had the roar of a lion, but the heart of a lamb. Since you never seemed to tire of talking and listening, I could always depend on you for communication, thus making my life less lonely.

Shortly before your demise, you thanked me for being your mother. I now thank God for lending you to me as a son.

~ Love Always,
Mom

CHAPTER 7

CHAPTER 7

Chrysler Corporation, which was nearby, was buying homes in our community because of expansion. Phil and I had been saving to buy a better home in a better area. So when Durand was three months old, my little family and I moved out of the ghetto. My aunt helped me to get a job as a maid, working for a white family in the suburbs. The husband and wife for whom I worked was friendly towards me that first Saturday. I only worked one day per week. When it was time for the lady with whom I rode to pick me up that first Saturday evening, I was ready. My bosses seemed especially interested in the fact that I had moved down the street from their friend in the city. When I went back on the following Saturday, I guess they had decided to put me "in my place." They were no longer friendly. I was given jobs that were not mentioned before as a part of my job description. In addition to cleaning the house, I had to wash windows, clean the basement and iron clothes. There was no lunch break, and no food was offered. When my ride came to pick me up, they were not finished working me. On that day, I felt that I was treated like less than a human being. When I left that day, I knew I would never go back. If I had continued working for them, it would have deflated my ego and lowered my self esteem. Shortly after that, I became pregnant again. My husband was usually nice to me when I was pregnant. However, that did not happen during my fifth pregnancy. Somehow I got through it. In September, I gave birth to a beautiful baby girl. Everybody was surprised and elated. Phil adored his little daughter.

At first, I didn't know what I was going to name her. Both Mona and I were pregnant at the same time. Mother wanted the next granddaughter to be named after Helena. The year before, Uncle Curtis and his wife had a baby daughter whom they named after Helena. So while Mona and I were both pregnant, we decided that we would not name a daughter, if we had one, after Helena; to do so, would be like disregarding our uncle's and aunt's baby's name. Both Mona and I agreed. So when Jeannie was born, I remembered what Mona and I had agreed upon. Therefore, I could only give her Helena's middle name, Jean. Mona was due to give birth one month before I was, but I gave birth six days before Mona did. Mona surprised me by calling me from the hospital to inform me that she was going to name her daughter Helena. I felt tricked. I had abided by our agreement. Mona said, "Making Mother happy is more important than what Uncle Curtis and Debbie think." I knew why she did it. She had said once before that the child named after Helena would be important to Mother. I never told her how I felt.

When Mona's baby and my baby were four months old, we decided to go back to high school in the evening and pursue a diploma. So we enrolled as eleventh graders. It had always bothered both Mona and me that we never even finished high school. My husband did not want me to go back to school. He told me, "There are two things you're never going to do again. You're not going to work, and you're not going back to school." He said "You're going to take care of these kids, this house, and take care of me." I don't know how I got the courage to defy him, but I did. My two older sons were too young to baby sit. Therefore, Mona would bring either her son, J. D. , or her daughter, Yvette, to baby sit for me each night. I paid them twenty-five cents per night.

Spring was upon us. Usually, my husband was a good financial provider. However, one year during the Easter season, I experienced something that I had not encountered before. It was the Saturday before Easter. My three sons, Beau, David and Lyle were in the Easter program at church. Each one had memorized his speech. It was my job to go out and shop for new clothing. Unfortunately, their father decided that he was not going to provide the money for Easter outfits. Those clothes were not just desired. The boys really needed them. I knew my spouse had the money because he had just gotten his pay check. Our income tax return check had also arrived. That was in his possession. He had agreed to lend my mother eighty dollars to shop for my little brother. But nothing was given toward shopping for our children. I was hurt and worried that Saturday. I needed someone to talk to. However, it could not have been a member of my family. I did not want my relatives to know that my spouse would not give me shopping money. Therefore, I called one of my favorite sisters-in-law who lived in Chicago. I was crying as I told her my problem. She asked, "What sizes do they wear?" I told her their sizes, but I also let her know that I did not expect her to help financially. I just needed someone with whom I could talk. That was about mid day on the Saturday before Easter. I accompanied my husband to Mother's house to give her the money she needed. My two sisters were there. They were going shopping for their children. They must have sensed that I was unhappy because someone said "What's wrong with you, Perseverance?" I replied "I have a headache." They must have believed me because no one mentioned it again. My sister, Lila wanted me to go shopping with her. I watched as Lila bought beautiful Easter outfits for her children. I had twenty one dollars, and three sons to shop for. I said to Lila, "My children don't need new outfits. So I'm just going to buy them socks and under clothes." I remembered that Lyle had a little brown necktie that he would have to wear. It was faded. So I bought brown shoe polish to cover the faded spots. When the shopping was over, Lila took me home. Before dawn that Easter morning, my husband's sister, Rose, called from the Greyhound bus station downtown for my husband to pick her up. After talking to me the day before, she used her pay check to buy Easter outfits for all three of my sons who were in the Easter

71

program. She had shopped for them in Chicago, caught the bus and made it to Detroit before day light on Easter morning with their clothes. That was an unexpected miracle. If I live to be a hundred, I shall never forget her for that. She had done lots of things for my husband, my children and me. But the good deed mentioned above, stands out most vividly. I owe her a debt of gratitude that I can never repay. I have told my children if their Aunt Rose ever needs them, I want them to be there for her. Some hurts and joys never go away. They just lie dormant. Writing about this experience was like reliving it. Therefore, once again, I wept while writing it.

After completing the eleventh grade in evening school, I discovered that I was pregnant with my sixth and youngest child, Shawny. It was a long hot summer. Various things happened, but one miracle stands out most vividly in my memory bank. During the summer of 1968, I had to pay my bill immediately, or the phone service would have been shut off. My husband and I had enough money in our savings account at Detroit Bank and Trust to pay the bill. However, the bank was many blocks from my home. I had to walk because I had no means of transportation. I was several months pregnant and was accompanied by my three year old son, Durand. We could not walk very fast and the bill had to be paid that day. It was already early afternoon, and the bank was scheduled to close at 3:00 p.m. My little son and I embarked upon our journey to the bank. I walked as swiftly as I could, and Durand was in a little trot. I prayed for the Lord to hold the doors of the bank open until we got there. As we walked, I saw a clock in the window of a store. It was already 3:00 p.m. I did not turn around to go back home. I just kept walking and praying, "Lord, hold the doors of the bank open until we get there." I did not know how the Lord was going to keep those doors open, but I knew that he was able to do so. The bank was closed when we got there, but I didn't turn around. Durand and I stood in front of the closed doors. A man who worked in the bank came to the door to inform me that the bank was closed. I said "I want to withdraw from my savings account to pay my telephone bill." The man told me to wait until he checked with someone else in the bank. On that day, the Lord got into the hearts and minds of the people in authority. They reopened the doors of the Detroit Bank and Trust to allow me to withdraw money from my savings account to pay my telephone bill. I was reminded that when God gets ready to move, no power on earth can stop Him! What a mighty God we serve!

Shawny was born that fall. When I came home from the hospital with the new baby, my three year old son, Durand was in training pants and two year old Jeannie was in diapers. Mother, who had taken care of them while I was in the hospital, must have felt sorry for me. She took Durand home with her. When he returned home, he was completely potty trained. I went back to school when Shawny was 2 weeks old because I wanted to graduate the following June. I did not neglect my duties as a wife and mother. I also did quite well academically. Mona's and my long range goal was to get a high school diploma. So the following June, we graduated from high school. Since I had acquired a hunger for knowledge, I thought, "Why not keep going?" Then I focused on a college degree as my goal. The summer and fall of 1969 was quite a memorable time for me. After graduating from Mumford High School that June, I enrolled in driver's training. I obtained my drivers license that summer. Afterwards, I talked to my friend, Sharon, about applying for college. Since she was a college student already, she was able to give me some valuable information. I applied and was accepted at Highland Park Community College. I remember how proud I was to see mail from a college with my name on it. Then came the difficult task. I had to ask Phil for the tuition I needed to pay for two classes. His answer was, "No." Fortunately, I had over heard him promise to give someone else much more than I asked for. Therefore, I pitched a fit. When I'd get really upset, I could complain for a long time. I guess I inherited that trait from Mama Lillie. Phil finally gave me the money for my tuition. That was a means of shutting me up; and so it did. I registered for two classes that fall and embarked upon a journey that was alien to my meager exposure to the academic world. Both my classes were taught in the evening. Since I had no intention of neglecting my duties at home, I usually took evening classes. After cooking dinner, I'd ride two buses to college. When classes were over, someone from my mother's side of the family would pick me up. I didn't dare ride buses home at night. Although my stepfather seemed indifferent when we were growing up, he made up for it by being so faithful in picking me up at night during those first two years in college. Whenever my stepfather could not pick me up, someone else in my family picked me up. My spouse would have nothing to do with how I got home at night. One night there was no one else to pick me up. Mother decided, as I talked to her on the phone, that she would call my husband and ask him to pick me up. She called him, but he would not come. However, he did tell her to tell me to get a cab; but I didn't want to ride in a cab alone at night. Finally, someone from my family came to pick me up. When my first semester in college was over, I was happy about my marks. I earned an "A" in one of my classes and a "B" in the other. When the second semester rolled around, I had no money to register for my classes. So I borrowed the money from a relative. I didn't tell Phil that I had borrowed money to continue attending college. My class was taught on Monday and Wednesday evenings. After I cooked dinner, I would catch two buses to college. My stepfather would pick me up when class was over at night. Since I did not want Phil to know that I had a class that semester, Dave would meet me at the door, take my books, and put them on the shelf in the vestibule closet. Then I would walk into the house, carrying only my purse. I wanted Phil to believe that I had been visiting my mother or one of my sisters. If he ever suspected that I was attending class, he never mentioned it. After that semester was over, I received financial aid for my tuition. Later, I received a Board of Governors Award when my grade point average was 3. 0 or better. I did not have to pay that back. Phil didn't take my education seriously. I guess he thought I was living in a fantasy world. When I took an Introduction to Speech Communication class, my instructor was impressed with my performance in class. She suggested that I change my major from Elementary Education to Speech. She said, "I think you will be good at it." I was excited when I went home and informed Phil of what my instructor had said. Phil replied, "Those people are making a fool out of you over there. They just want your money." Nevertheless, I switched my major to Speech. I applied for financial aid, which paid my tuition. I had to go full time then. My classes were still given in the evening.

When I graduated from Highland Park Community College with an Associate Degree, Phil did not come, but other members of my family came. During commencement, I looked at my former instructors and thought of the academic contribution each one had made to me. There were two instructors to whom I was most grateful. Mr. Wilx taught Physical Science. The course could have been difficult and boring, but he made it easier and interesting. We would go to his class with our thick 3-4 subject notebooks and pens, as we did for other classes, prepared to take notes during most of our time there. Instead of allowing us to write, write, write all during his lecture, he would give notes and an example for each note. Then he'd say, "Now write." By that time, the information given was already embedded within our memory banks. The other instructor was Mrs. Knowles. She taught Speech Communication. Many black students thought she was prejudice. If she was, I never saw that side of her character. She always treated me with respect and admiration. When I was no longer her student, I would sometimes see her in the hallway or in the cafeteria accompanied by someone else. She would introduce me to whomever she was with, and tell them what a good student I was, how many children I had, and that she wished she had more students like me. It was she who encouraged me to change my major from Elementary Education to Speech. In addition to being a terrific Speech Communication instructor, Mrs. Knowles contributed to the regaining of my self confidence. There were still many difficulties that I faced at home while pursuing my Associate Degree. Phil's two brothers, Joseph and Richard moved to Detroit from Mississippi. They came to live with Phil and me. Richard came during the summer. Although he was bossy at times, he had a kind heart. We all got along fine. One Christmas, Richard went down South to visit for the holidays. When he returned, he brought Joseph back with him from Mississippi to live with us also. Joseph had an outgoing personality, but he was mean. For some reason, he seemed to have developed a dislike for me. My study habits began to suffer. Sometimes while studying, I would realize that I was thinking of Richard and Joseph instead of my studies. I began to have headaches, and my legs became so weak at times; they seemed to tremble as I went up and down the stairs. I knew that I could not depend on my husband's support. He would fight me on the issue. One Saturday I went to the library. When I returned home, Joseph and Richard had rearranged every piece of furniture in my living room. That was too much. My husband had never done that. After observing the blatant action of my brothers-in-law, I asked them to move. When Phil came home, I informed him that I had asked his brothers to move. Phil did not say anything to me. He went into his brothers' room to talk with them. I tried to eavesdrop from our room across the hall. However, I was unable to hear what was said. I expected them to move right away, but as time went on, my headaches continued. Once while talking to Phil's older sister, Marian, about the situation, she replied, "Phil may have told them that they don't have to move. Billy, (Marian's husband) and I were talking, and Billy said Phil is suppose to be supporting his wife." I knew that Marian loved all of her brothers but she loved me enough to be fair. Some months later, Richard moved back down South. Before leaving he came to me and said, "Thank you for all you have done for me." His expression of gratitude made me feel better. Joseph continued to stay on. He also continued to be arrogant. One day as he was about to leave for work, I called him into my room and said, "I'm going to give you one month to move. If you are not gone by then, I'm going to take action myself." That ultimatum was spoken with neither kindness nor meanness. However, I did speak with firmness. The ultimatum did the job. Joseph moved within a week, without saying good-bye, I'm gone, or anything. I felt better as I resumed my studies and life with my spouse and children. Today, I have great admiration for men who love, honor and respect their wives. Life was already stressful enough without family members adding to it.

During those days, blacks had to deal with the harassment of stress cops and uniform police officers on the streets of Detroit. One evening the cops picked up my nephew, J. D. After putting him into the police car, the officers tried to persuade him to make a run for his freedom. J. D. thought they wanted an excuse to shoot him. So he refused to get out and run. I thank God J. D. was thinking clearly. I remember another terrifying encounter that my fourteen year old son, Phil Jr. and I had with some Detroit cops during the beginning of the 1970s. My son and I had been visiting my sister-in-law. Shortly after we left Marian's house one night, I noticed that two white men were following us. I had no way of knowing that they were stress cops because they were driving an unmarked car and wearing plain clothes. I was frightened. They followed us for several blocks. I lived more than two miles away, so I decided to drive to my sister, Mona's house. We were going to jump out of my car and run into Mona's house. When I turned the corner, about two and a half blocks from my sister's home, marked police cars pulled up, blocking us from the front and side. I realized then that the two plain clothes men in the unmarked car behind us, must have been STRESS cops. They had not identified themselves as they followed us. I stopped the car. We were ordered to get out of the car with hands up. A number of uniformed police officers had guns drawn on my son and me. It was terrifying to feel that at any given moment, one of those guns might go off, or one of the cops may get trigger happy. Two African American women who observed what was happening, asked if there was anyone whom I wanted them to call for me. I suggested my brother and thanked them for their concern. One male stress cop frisked me. Other cops had my son against a tree frisking him. They were all in my car like animals. As one of the stress cops probed through my purse, he seemed to have gotten excited when he found a pill. His enthusiasm dwindled however, when I said, "That's nothing but a Di-gel tablet for indigestion." The cops' excuse for their actions was "We suspected your son of being involved in a shoot-out on Burlingame."My driver license was returned to me after they discovered that we were squeaky clean. Finally, they let us go without an apology. By that time I was very nervous. However, I was blessed to have been able to drive home safely. I thought "What a terrifying experience; and what a waste of the tax payers' money. If everyone was like me, there would be no need for police." I thank God for those marked police cars pulling up before my son and I reached my sister's house. I shudder to think of what those stress cops would have done to my son and me if we had begun to run for my sister's house. I also shudder to think of the many innocent people who have met their fate at the hands of unbalanced, insensitive trigger-happy police officers.

I was informed of my acceptance to Wayne State University. When fall came, my classes began with me as a junior. I declared Speech Pathology as my major. Science was my minor. Once again, I arranged to attend classes in the evening so that I would not have to neglect my duties at home with my family. Phil Jr. and David helped out a lot by baby sitting for me. Immediately after cooking dinner in the evening, I would catch the bus to the university. I asked my stepfather to pick me up at night, just as he had when I attended Highland Park Community College. He did not fail me. When classes were over, my ride was there waiting for me. However, I noticed that he was riding with my brother-in-law. I realized why he had gotten someone else to pick me up; though I never mentioned it. By that time my stepfather was an old man. The University campus was huge. Thus, it was more difficult for him to find his way around. So after that first night, I never asked Mr. Sam to pick me up after class again. I promised my stepdad that after I graduated and got a job, I would not forget him. Other arrangements had to be made pertaining to how I would get home from school at night. Sometimes I would take either David or Lyle with me in the evening. He, (whichever one it was), would wait in the university library for me. After classes were over, we would ride the bus together. Therefore, I did not have to walk those long dark blocks home alone after I got off the bus at night. Beau baby sat for me. Sometimes I would ride the bus to the university alone. David would meet me at the bus stop at night. He would wait for me in a restaurant across the street from the bus stop. Then we would walk home together. Looking back, I do not know how I would have made it without God's help, my family, and my two eldest sons, Beau and David. Surely I owe a debt of gratitude that I can never repay. Beau and David stood by me through thick and thin. Even though they were quite young, they sure tried to make my life easier for me. Usually I had bus fare when I was in college. However, there were times when I had no bus fare. On those occasions, Beau and David would take turns taking a bag lunch every other day, and giving me their lunch money for my bus fare to the university. Phil always gave them lunch money each morning before leaving for work. We never told him of the financial contribution my sons made toward my education.

During the first day of every class, I always introduced myself to someone, and we exchanged telephone numbers. Thus, if one of us was absent, the other could share notes by phone. Several of us studied together and became a close knit little group. I made more friends while attending the university, than during any other period in my life. Speech Pathology was interesting and challenging. "Introduction to Speech Correction," one of my first classes at the university was especially exciting. In addition to other requirements for the course, we had to do 30 hours of observation of speech therapy. Therefore, I observed at various hospitals, speech and hearing clinics and schools. It was fascinating and touching as I observed therapy for patients who had speech impediments due to various causes. The patients ranged in ages from the very young to the very old. I loved my major. During the second semester, I met my "waterloo." I took a course entitled "Theories of Normal Language Development." The title of the text book was *Psycho Linguistics.* The author of that book was so deep. Even with the help of a dictionary, I could not understand the meaning of the text. Comprehension fled from me. I felt that I was lost within an academic world that I knew nothing about. Each time I turned a paper in, I received a failing grade. It was a large class which consisted of a majority of non blacks. There were some sharp minds in that class. Unfortunately, I did not understand. I was glad the instructor did not single people out to call upon during class discussions. He did not have to do so. There were always those who volunteered answers. One day, as the instructor was passing papers back, he gave me my "E" paper and said "Perseverance, if you're having trouble with this course, you should come in to see me because some of your answers are way out." He said it loudly enough for everyone nearby to hear. I was so embarrassed, I felt like going through the floor. One young lady who was seated nearby, looked at me with pity in her eyes, and said, "I'll help you." I thanked her. However, I had a better idea. I was reminded that wisdom belongs to God. I went home that evening, took out my text book and kneeled down on my knees. My prayer was, "Lord, open up my understanding." After that, every paper I turned in was an "A" paper. I don't remember getting even a "B" paper. The instructor gave us one opportunity to improve our grades. Since my grades had leaped from "E's" to "A's," my instructor replaced all of my failing grades in his record book with "A's." He told me, near the end of the semester, that no one in class was doing better than I. Truly the Lord had opened up my understanding. But God still had something to reveal to my instructor, my peers, and to me. You see, God remembered that day when I was embarrassed in class. So God did not stop at opening up my understanding and changing my grades from "E's" to "A's. He proceeded to erase my embarrassment in the presence of the class and let me know how much he had opened my understanding. Finally, it was time to review for the final exam. The instructor asked the class what message was the author trying to convey to the reader in chapter one. Many students raised their hands and attempted to answer. But not one of them knew the answer. As usual, I did not volunteer because I had no idea that I knew the answer. Then the instructor did something that had not been characteristic of him. He singled out someone to call upon for the answer. He said, "Perseverance, what message is the author trying to convey to the reader in chapter one?" As a means of stalling, I said "Would you repeat that question, please?" Once again he asked, "What message is the author trying to convey to the reader in chapter one?" Knowing that I could stall no longer, I said, "Thought and language are not one and the same, but yet they can't be separated." The instructor seemed to have been both excited and relieved as he said, "That's it!" My final mark for the course was an "A."

During the summer semester at Wayne State University, I took a class with a very unreasonable instructor. I can't say that she was prejudice because many students of various races were having problems with her. I would readily have dealt with her for one semester. However, I discovered that I would have to take another course with her as an instructor. I no longer wanted to continue in Speech Pathology. Yet I did not want to lose the credit hours I had acquired during the past year. Therefore, I talked with my advisor about changing majors. I discovered that all courses that were taken in Speech Path were equivalent to certain courses in Speech Communication. Therefore, Speech Communication became my new major. I was able to keep all of the credit hours that I had acquired, even Audiology, and I loved Speech Communication as much as I had loved Speech Pathology. My minor also changed. At Wayne State, if one chose Speech Communication as a major, he/she had to minor in English. That caused me to have to take a number of courses in my minor. That was not a problem for me because English had always been my favorite subject. So I was into both a major and minor that I truly loved. Speech Communication not only enhanced my speaking ability, it contributed to the regaining of my self confidence that I had lost many years before.

There was quite a transportation problem during my university years. Many nights I was alone and did not know how I would get home. Panic would set in when most other students had gone. They would begin locking the university doors, and I had no ride home. During my junior year, an incident occurred that is embedded within my memory bank as if it was a photograph in motion. I thought I had another ride home. Therefore, I did not tell my son, David to meet me at the bus stop that night. Near nine o'clock, I discovered that I had no ride. The campus building attendant where I had a class, had already locked the doors. The last Second Avenue bus ran a little past nine. I had to catch that bus, and yet I was afraid to walk those long dark blocks home alone after getting off the bus. The nearest place that was open was a restaurant near campus. I remember running that night, trying to call David to tell him to meet me at the bus stop. So I went into the restaurant and asked a white lady, who seemed to have been in charge, if I could pay to use her phone. She refused. Then I said, "Can I give you the money for the call and my home phone number? Just tell David to meet me at the bus stop." That white lady never said a word. She just sat there starring at me with her eyes wide. I turned and left the restaurant, running to the bus stop. I knew I had to catch that last bus. I had to take my chances walking home from the bus stop alone. Fortunately, a lady who lived on the next block from me, was on the bus. Her son met her at the bus stop. We all walked home together that night. There were some rough, terrifying times. But the word "quit" never entered my mind. Thank God, I made it!

 **C**HAPTER **8**

CHAPTER 8

During the winter quarter of my senior year at Wayne State, I did my student teaching. That was a time I had looked forward to, but yet dreaded. I had a fear of getting an unfair critic teacher. Since I had heard so many negative stories about my peers' critic teachers, I was leery. The night before reporting to my assigned school, I was filled with anxiety. Sleep fled from me. On the following morning, I reported to Murray-Wright High School for my student teaching assignment. My critic teacher was Linda James. She was a nice, no nonsense white woman who was ten years my junior. Getting to school was difficult because I had to ride three buses and get there before eight o'clock in the morning. Since my student teaching assignment was from January to April, I had to catch two buses while it was still dark out side. The thought of standing at the bus stops before the dawning of the day was terrifying. Phil had two cars at that time. When I asked about using that second car, he said it was not insured. Having no money of my own with which to purchase auto insurance and tags, I resorted to catching those three buses in order to get to and from school each day. Fortunately, I did not have to wait at the first two bus stops alone for long. My cousin, who taught at another high school downtown, needed a place to live. So he called and asked if he could stay with us for a few months. My spouse and I agreed to allow him to live with us for a brief period. Roger, my cousin, had no car either. Therefore, we rode the first two buses together in the morning. By the time I caught the third bus alone, I was not afraid because it was day light. Once each school day was over, catching the buses home in the evening was an ordeal. It was a very cold winter. Many times, the buses would pass those of us up at the bus stop because the buses were already filled to capacity. By the time I got home, I would feel as though I was chilled to the bone. I'd change into warm casual clothing and get into bed until my body was warm. Then I would go downstairs and cook dinner. Linda was a great critic teacher. She was intelligent, nice and fair. But I knew If I did not do my job, she would can me. I was to observe her in the classroom for one week before taking over three classes myself. As a means of keeping me focused while she was teaching, she would encourage students to ask for my input during class discussions. Sometimes, while I was still observing, she would suddenly mention something she had to do, and ask, "Perseverance, would you take over the class?" She made me a part of what was going on while she taught. Thus, she kept me constantly on my toes. By the end of my student teaching contact, both Linda and I had learned to love and respect each other.

During the spring quarter, I registered for my last three classes that were geared toward June graduation. While I was preparing to graduate from college, Beau was preparing to graduate from high school. My graduation was such a grand occasion for me. Several members of my family were there. They were excited. You see, I was the first member of my immediate family to ever graduate from college. I kept thinking, "I made it!" Unfortunately, Phil did not attend the commencement as I received a Bachelor of Science Degree in Education, from Wayne State University. Summer was upon us. Phil gave that second car I wanted to a member of his family. I was neither hurt nor angry. I went about the business of looking for a job in the teaching profession. That was a good summer except for one tragic incident. Evan, a friend of my son, David, was shot and killed on the next block from my home. Another young man shot him because of a $10.00 debt. My children came in the house and told me that he was lying on the street. However, neither they nor I knew that he was dead.

We walked around the corner to the crime scene. There I saw Evan lying on the street. Flies had already begun to swarm around his body as family members stood around crying. Then came one of the worst moments. The victim's mom, who was not around when the shooting took place, came down the street where the crowd was gathered. When she asked what happened, someone replied, "Evan was shot, and he just died." My feelings were indescribable. I turned, gathered my children, and went home to take a tranquilizer, and climbed into bed.

Although my marriage was not a happy one, Phil had many admirable qualities. He definitely believed in God. Even though he stopped attending church for quite a while, he would play only spiritual music on his guitar. Neither his children, nor I ever heard him use profanity. Economically, he provided well for his family. He was generous and dependable. He would lend money to anyone in need. I have seen him lend money to people he didn't even like. He could not say "No" to anyone in need. He was a kind man to almost everyone. Unfortunately, Phil's kindness did not extend to me. He had a strong resentment for me which never seemed to go away. During all the years we were married, I heard him say something positive about me only once. It was during the first few years of our marriage. I was seated behind the steering wheel of his car. He looked at me and said, "You look nice behind the wheel of that car." For the rest of our married life, I never heard another compliment. Most of our time together consisted of non-communication or complaints. I am a very good cook, but if he ever enjoyed a meal, he never told me so. He never told me that I looked nice, no matter how much I groomed myself. Phil always seemed miserable with me. I eventually came to the conclusion that Phil thought he was in love with me when we married, but he realized later that what he felt for me was not real love. Therefore, he was miserable and frustrated. There was almost no communication between him and our children either. They longed for a relationship with him. I talked to them a lot. However, that could never make up for the lack of communication between them and their father. Beau and David lived that life with me during those very difficult years. Since they were older, they understood more about what life was like in our home. I used to send them to ask their dad for money for me. It made me nervous to hear the mean tone of his voice when he said, "No." So I would stand out of his way, with my fingers in my ears as they asked for money. Sometimes he would voluntarily leave spending money for us in the morning, before leaving for work. However, he would hide the money. So Beau, David and I would have to search for it. It would be hidden under any number of objects within our home. Usually, we would find it. There were days when I'd wonder if there was money hidden that we did not find. During those times when I experienced gross mistreatment and disrespect, my self esteem sank to bottom level. But I also underwent another change. There were occasions when I was walking down the street, sitting in church, or in other public places, I'd have a great urge to burst into tears. However, I knew that would have drawn the attention of others around me. So I controlled my emotions. Only in the privacy of my home could I unleash that fountain of suppressed tears.

I was thankful to have my sons. Both Beau and David were very sensitive, caring young men. They were obedient when they were growing up. Yet both of them turned to drugs after they grew up. Neither of their younger siblings did. I know that every man is responsible for his own actions; and "the fittest will survive." Nevertheless, I can't help wondering if their lives would have turned out differently had their dad developed a positive rapport with them. Although I was happy about my academic accomplishment, my self- esteem was still low, and I undervalued myself. You see, I felt unloved by the most important man in the world to me. Nothing seemed too harsh for my husband to say to me. Once when we were not even arguing, Phil said to me, "I don't have any desire for you. I wouldn't care if you had another man right here in this house!" I think those words hurt more than a physical beating would have. After experiencing much verbal abuse myself, I taught my children to never hit below the belt during an argument with their spouses. I cautioned them to never verbalize their whole mind if their thoughts could hurt someone else. I informed them that once cruel words come out of your mouth and fall on the listener's ears, you can never take them back, and the person to whom you're speaking, may never be able to forget those words.

Finally, I decided that I was not going to take verbal abuse anymore without speaking up for myself. I was reminded of a quote from Shakespeare's *Julius Caesar*. After having been warned to beware the Ides of March, Caesar's response to his wife's plea to stay home, was, "Cowards die many times before their death. The valiant never taste of death but once." I decided to take a tip from that quote as a starting point pertaining to my courage. When I first began to speak up for myself, Phil told me that I needed to see a psychiatrist. I discovered that during arguments, I could be louder than Phil. Speaking up did not enhance our relationship and arguments weren't good for me spiritually. However, I did not undervalue myself as much.

 **CHAPTER 9**

CHAPTER 9

The summer of 1975 was over. I was hired by Detroit Board of Education. My first teaching assignment was at Greusel Middle School, the school that I had graduated from more than twenty years before. The administrators were delighted to have a teacher who had graduated from Greusel. Students called me "Kotter," as in the television show *Welcome Back Kotter*. It was ironic that the classroom that was assigned to me as an English teacher was the same room that I had English classes in as a student back in the 1950s. For a while, I enjoyed being there. Soon I realized that I really preferred teaching in the senior high school. So after having taught at Greusel for three months, I accepted a teaching position at Murray-Wright High, the school where I did my student teaching. My first position at Murray-Wright was working as a substitute teacher in the Home Economics Department. I taught in the above department for one semester. The following fall, I was assigned to teach in an English position. That made me happy because I was working toward a contract. One had to teach in an area that he/ she was certified in, for one hundred consecutive days in order to get a contract. I'm certified to teach Speech and English, grades 9-12. After teaching in that position for about eighty days, I felt confident that I would make the one hundred days and get my contract. You see, my former critic teacher was there. She had proven to be a dear friend to me. The administrators thought I was competent. Therefore, I figured getting a contract was a matter of twenty days away. However, the Lord showed me that I was absolutely powerless without his help.

On a Friday, during semester break, Mrs. Sneet, an assistant principal, called me into the office. She informed me that on the following Monday, a contract teacher at large would be coming to Murray-Wright to fill the English vacancy that I held. He had first priority because he already had a contract. The man was coming from another high school in the city. I went into the principal's office to talk to him. I just cried. The principal, Bryce Bower, was sympathetic, but said he was unable to do anything about the situation. I later remembered the source of all power. I began to pray. My prayer was "Lord, please don't let that man take my job." Later, I changed my prayer to "Lord, if it's your will, don't let him take my job. But if it's your will for him to get the job, fix me so that I won't worry about it." I knew the Lord could see the future, but I could not. I called Mother on the phone while at school that Friday. I told her what happened and asked her to pray for me. Mother said, "I'm going on a fast, and you fast too." So that Saturday, both Mother and I went on a fast. On the following Monday, I returned to work only to find that the contract teacher at large had my job. I was assigned to substitute teach in an English-Social Studies position. I could never have gotten a contract with that split schedule because I was not certified to teach Social Studies. However, God had fixed my heart and mind so that I did not worry about losing my position. During the early afternoon that Monday, Mrs. Sneet called over the P. A. for me to come to the main office. When I arrived in the office, the assistant principal was talking to Mr. Roberts, the man who bumped me. I learned that he had decided to go on sick leave. Mrs. Sneet was quite angry. She asked Mr. Roberts, a middle aged white man, "Did you know you were going on sick leave when you accepted this position?" He answered, "No." Mrs. Sneet asked, "How long will you be gone?" I stood there silently, hoping he would not give a specific time for returning to work. To my delight, Mr. Roberts answered, in an indifferent tone, "I have no idea." I was told that the man left before the day was over. The head secretary told me that Mr. Bower, the principal, telephoned the region office pertaining to the situation. She quoted Mr. Bower as saying "I had an excellent teacher in that position; and you sent me a fool out here!" So God put it on Mr. Roberts' heart and mind to go on sick leave, and leave on the same day he came. On the next day, the administrators put me back into my English position. Soon afterward, I got my contract. That was the position I retired from on February 1, 1999.

Teaching was a great fulfillment for me. Correct grammatical usage of the English language had been important to me ever since I was that little poverty stricken girl in the second grade. My friend, Jackie, said I made literature come alive. When introducing a novel or short story, I would briefly discuss a personal situation either about my life, or the life of someone I knew which related to the story. I would also instruct students to think over their lives, or the life of a relative or friend who experienced a similar situation as the characters within the story. I believed that if my students could identify with characters and situations in a story, it would stimulate their interest and enhance comprehension. Happiness was beginning to stare me in the face. I was able to tune out some of my marital problems at home.

Mona was getting prepared to graduate from W. S. U. with a Bachelor of Science Degree in Education. Mother was so proud to see yet another daughter who had struggled up from the cotton fields of Tennessee, accept her college degree. Mona had eight children at the time. Aunt Estelle, who had no children of her own, always attended our graduation. She also was proud. She used to show our graduation pictures to the white people for whom she worked. Lila, who had three children, also went back to pursue a college degree. Unfortunately, she had to give up her dream. After three years, Lila dropped out of college because of failing health and marital problems. Lila's rough plight was far from being over. Finally, she decide to leave him. Somehow he heard about her moving date. Therefore as a means of safety precaution, Lila decided that she would not move anytime near that date. She waited until he thought she had changed her mind. When her husband had gone to work one day, Lila had a moving van pull up in front of her house. With her gun available, she began to move. Friends and relatives helped her. Jim's best friend, Louis, who lived down the street, came out on his porch to see what was happening. Lila said to her daughter, Lucy, "Call Louis and tell him if he tells Jim I'm moving, he (Louis) is going to die this day because I'm going to kill him!" So Lila stepped away from her marriage that day to embark upon a new direction in life.

During the following fall, Mona accepted a job as substitute teacher at the school where I worked. I loved the fact that we were working together. However, a few petty minded staff members did not like the idea that both Mona and I worked together. Some even compared our personalities and decided that my sister was not as friendly as I. I explained that once people get to know my sister, they would find that she's a wonderful person. Winter was upon us. It was time to do my Christmas shopping. For the first time, I planned to give a gift to J. D. and Yvette, the nephew and niece who baby sat my children for twenty five cents per night, while I pursued a high school diploma. During that time, J. D. was having a difficult time with his live-in girlfriend. Mona had a bad feeling about her son's relationship with that young woman. Even though J. D. was twenty-three years old, my sister pleaded with him to get away from Lois, his girlfriend. Early on Christmas morning, J. D. arrived home and found his live-in girlfriend in bed with another man. The other man shot and killed J. D. That Christmas was not a merry one for our family. Mona was so pitiful. Twenty- three years have passed, but I still have flash backs of a person on each side of Mona, gently pulling her toward her son's casket on the evening we went to the funeral home to see if his body was ready for viewing by the general public. My sister was screaming and pulling back as the person on each side of her held her hand. Finally, the funeral was over and so was the Christmas season. When I returned to work, Mona returned also. She wanted to keep busy. She kept up such a brave front at school. I felt sorry for her because I knew she was hurting inwardly. With God's help, she made it through the rest of the school year.

Summer vacation was here. Although Mona tried to be brave after the death of her eldest son, there was a sadness about her that never seemed to go away. During late July of that year, Mona and her husband went on a trip to Chicago. I agreed to take care of her two youngest children, twelve year old Helena Amora and six year old Andre, who was also my godson. After a few days, Mona and her husband returned home. She talked with the kids on the night of her return. However, I kept the children with me that Sunday night. On Monday morning Andre told me that he had a stomach ache, and wanted to go home. So I took him and his sister home. When he got out of the car, he looked back at me and said "Bye." I had no idea that would be our last good-bye. On Wednesday night, Mona called me and said Andre' wasn't acting as cheerful as he usually did, and he was lying around a lot. Whenever she questioned him about how he felt, he would tell her that he felt okay. Nevertheless, Mona had decided to take him to the doctor on the following day. Before dawn that Thursday morning, Andre woke her up and told her that he couldn't breathe. Mona and her husband took him to Children's Hospital immediately. He was talking, and even walked into the hospital on his own, but little Andre died that day before the doctor examined him. He went into cardiac arrest. The doctors said he had inflammation of the heart muscles. My sister was so pitiful. She was in a state of shock. She had lost her eldest son and her youngest son within seven months. I did not allow Mona to go back home when she left the hospital that morning. I took her home with me. She was hurting so badly, and yet I felt inadequate to comfort her. I wanted either Mona's husband, or my mother to be there at all times. She seemed to need more comfort than I knew how to give. After the funeral was over, my sister and her husband went back home. She began to try to pick up the pieces and go on with her life. She told me years later that her life was separated into two eras. One era was before the death of her sons, and the other was after their death.

CHAPTER 10

Sometimes Cliff, a young man who attended high school with me, would telephone me. Although Phil had never met him, it was okay that he called once in a while. I had explained to my husband who he was. Cliff and I had been friends since I was sixteen years old. When we were in high school, he was a friend of Leonard's, a fellow I used to date then. I neither dated Cliff, nor did he ever ask for a date. We were only friends. It was through a poem he wrote for me, while I was yet sixteen, he revealed that his interest in me surpassed friendship. However, he never verbalized his feelings. Whenever Cliff called, I would talk to him in the den, whether Phil was present or not, since my husband knew we were only friends. One evening my daughter answered the phone when Cliff called. I told my daughter to hang up the phone downstairs when I picked up upstairs. I decided to take the call upstairs that time because I wanted to discuss a personal problem with him. My husband must have become suspicious because I chose to talk in private that day. Phil took the phone from our daughter, Shawny, and eavesdropped. After the conversation was over, I started back down stairs. I never got past the top of the stairs. Phil was climbing those stairs, two at a time. When he got to the top of the stairs, he reached out and grabbed me by the throat. He ushered me back to our bedroom and asked in an angry tone, "Who was that man you were talking to? I will kill you!" I told him who it was and reminded him that we were only talking about food. I decided to postpone talking to Cliff about my personal problem. Since Phil eavesdropped, he knew I was telling the truth. However, he said, "I could tell the conversation was going to get heavy." I called my eldest son, Beau. I was scared because he still had me by the throat. Beau came and stood in our doorway. He asked, "Mom, are you all right?" His daddy said to him, "Go on back downstairs!" However, Beau did not go back downstairs. He just stood there in the doorway watching us. Finally, Phil let go of me. While eavesdropping on my conversation with my friend, he heard Cliff tell me that I could talk to him about anything. For a while after that, Phil actually listened to me when I talked. He even said to me once, "You can tell me what's on your mind." We got along much better for a while. Laughingly, I told Cliff that he did wonders for my marriage. Later, I told Phil's sister Marion, who was a dear friend of mine, what had happened. She laughed heartily. She knew her brother had been acting like the big bad wolf who really did not want me for years.

Chapter 11

During the summer when my daughter, Jeannie, was nine years old, she accompanied her father down South to visit his family. Phil's family lived in the rural area of Mississippi. My husband's siblings and their children had gathered from far and near for the reunion. I thought Jeannie would have an enjoyable time, even though I did not go, nor did any of her siblings. That was her first trip to her dad's hometown. When Jeannie and her father returned home, she did not say much about her trip. A short time later, I noticed that Jeannie had written something in my notebook pertaining to her trip. She wrote, "When I was in Mississippi, Aunt Joan thought I stole her money." I foolishly believed that my daughter only assumed her aunt thought she was guilty of stealing her money. I failed to realize then that her writing that in my notebook symbolized her little plea for help. I now feel that I failed my daughter by neglecting to ask questions and discuss the incident immediately. It was not until seven years later, that Jeannie told her sister-in-law and me what really happened between her Aunt Joan and her.

She said to us, "I couldn't believe my father had said I could go along with him on his trip. I really don't know what made me ask, but when I told my mother I wanted to go to Mississippi with my father, I expected them to say no or maybe next time. Instead she came back to the den after discussing it with my father, and quickly brushed my hair so that I could go to the mall with her to get me some clothes to wear on my trip. I remembered my dad taking trips to Mississippi before without us, to visit his family.

And I remembered his family members coming to visit our house over the years. All of those memories were wonderful. There were so many smiling faces at the dinner tables my mother prepared for them. One could say that her table matched that of a king's during a feast. There were china, silverware and crystal glasses that I never saw until they came to visit us. When we returned from the mall, I ran up stairs to show my sister the outfits my mother had bought for me. I had never been so excited in my life. This was my first trip out of town. And we were going to see all of my dad's brothers and sisters who filled our house with happy spirits every year. I always felt like I was more like my father's side of the family, and fitting in would be no problem. I hardly slept on the way down there. All I kept thinking about was how happy those same people were going to be when they saw me, and how I was going to wear my favorite outfit that my mother had bought for me. It was a white short jumper set with a multi color T-shirt. I thought to myself, "That will be the first outfit I'll wear there" I had been told by other adults that I looked a lot like my father. And sometimes I felt like I was his favorite child. Oh I was more than ready to visit his family.

When we arrived at Aunt Emma's house that sat back far from the road, the house was filled with people and beds. There were beds in every room of the house. I stood real close to my father while he walked through the crowd of people. As they hugged and kissed him, they would gently pat me on the head and say hello. The atmosphere was just as I had imagined it would be. Everyone was very excited to see my dad. Their conversations were filled with screams and laughter. They finally noticed that I was clinging to my father and my aunt Joan asked me to go in the back with the other children who had been peeking around the corner at me the whole time. The children seemed to cling to me. I could tell that they liked me a lot. I remember asking them where the bathroom was, and they escorted me outside to what looked like a small closet outdoors. It was very dark and all I could hear were crickets, frogs and what sounded like snakes slithering. There was no way I was going in there. I kept saying that it went away and I didn't have to use it anymore. As I lay on the pallet with the other kids, I kept squeezing my legs and stomach to keep from using the bathroom on myself. Hours had passed, and the house was silent. I jumped up because I couldn't hold it any longer. I went to the back door and looked out to where the outhouse stood, which from the distance, looked like part of the woods it stood near. I was more scared of going out there than using it on myself. So I stepped out the door, pulled my pants down, and used it on the porch. I could hear someone walking around in the front room. So I quickly ran back to the pallet. Moments later, my aunt Emma came walking by with some rags in her hand. I was so afraid that she was going to step out the door into the wet spot. When she got to the door, she leaned over with the rags and wiped clean the wet spot. I knew I was in for it then. She had seen me. Why didn't I just go out to the outhouse? There was no way out of this one. I couldn't go back to sleep now. A few hours later everyone started getting up and I just lay there, even after all the kids had gotten up, because I was afraid she was going to be angry with me. Instead, she came and got me up, gave me a hug and walked me out to the outhouse. She stood there with me until I was finished. Then she walked me back to the house and told me to come and get her when I got ready to use the bathroom. She was really kind to me. She made sure that I had everything I needed while I was there.

Later that evening, everyone went over to my aunt Christine's house. Her home was a lot more modern. It had a bathroom, and different areas of the house that we could walk through. We were told to go into one of the bedrooms to play. We were jumping up and down on the bed, tickling each other, throwing pillows, screaming and having a good time. Suddenly the door flung open and my aunt Joan asked everyone to leave the room but me. I thought to myself, "She couldn't be upset about the noise in here because we were all making noise. Maybe my aunt Emma told her about the incident that occurred this morning." "Where's my money?" she screamed. "What money?" I responded. "You know what money I'm talking about." I stood there looking up at her very mean looking face as she was talking to me. "I don't know what money you are talking about." She took her index finger and kept poking me in the chest while yelling at me, "You had better give me my money or I'm going to beat your behind." She grabbed me by my shoulders and shook me continuously while saying "I want my eleven dollars, and I mean it." After she let go, she told me to empty my pockets. I thought that she would calm down once I had emptied my pockets, but that seemed to have made her more angry. As she went to the door, she replied, You had better give me my money and I mean it, and don't come out of this room!" As I sat there on the bed, I kept thinking to myself, "Why would she say I had her money?" I had no idea what she was talking about. Why was she so angry with me? It was more than a look of anger, it was hatred in her eyes. I thought maybe she went out to fuss at the other children now, maybe she'll scold them as she scolded me." Moments later the other children came back into the room. I asked my cousin Alice, "Was Aunt Joan fussing at you all?" "No," responded Alice, "I just heard her telling Momma nem you took some money out of her purse." When they called us out for dinner, I could tell that everyone was looking at me very funny. I kept looking around for my dad but he must have stepped out for something. I had never felt so uncomfortable in my life. None of the adults were saying anything to me, but they kept chatting with the other children. After I ate, I went back into the bedroom where no one could look at me solemnly. After a while, I could hear my dad talking, so I came back out into the living room where everyone was sitting. As I glanced over at my Aunt Joan to see if she was still angry, she rolled her eyes harder than a pair of dice. If looks could kill, I would have died right there on the spot. Instead of sitting near my dad, I kept walking towards the front door because for some reason I knew what that look meant that she gave me. It was almost as if to say, "GET OUT!" I sat on the porch wishing that everyone would hurry up so that we could go back to Aunt Emma's house. I felt more comfortable there. I remembered that hug she gave me, it was real. If my dad tried to leave again, I would jump in the car with him for sure. I wasn't going to let him leave me alone again. There was no more whispering going on since my father returned. Now all I could hear was laughter again.

After a while Aunt Joan, Aunt Delia and Aunt Marva came out and headed back to Aunt Emma's. I felt a little more comfortable there, now that they were gone. It wasn't long before we were headed back to Aunt Emma's also. When we got there, we were told to get ready for bed. When I went to my suitcase to get my pajama's, everything in my bag was tossed everywhere. My socks were pulled away from each other, my clothes were unfolded and scrambled everywhere, and the suitcase itself was left unlocked. Did she really think I stole her money? Why had she gone through all of my things this way? What did I do to make her think I took her money? Why did she look at me with hatred in her eyes? What did I do? The next morning I got up and put my favorite outfit on. "I thought, "They will not be mad at me when they see how cute I look in this new outfit my mother bought for me." I was too afraid to ask Aunt Emma to go out to the outhouse with me. Aunt Joan may have gotten to her and told her that I took some money from her. My cousin, Pat, showed me where everyone else used the bathroom at night. There was a room sitting off of the front porch with a bucket full of waste and urine in it. I went in and used the bathroom. As I walked out the room, I thought to myself, "Hey that bucket is almost full. Maybe if I empty the bucket for them, they will be proud of me and not angry." I grabbed the bucket and carried it down the front porch and on to the side of the house. As I walked, splashes from the bucket got on my new jumper set, but I didn't care, I was more excited about them being glad that I emptied the bucket than I was my outfit. The bucket was almost heavier than I was. When I got to the back of the house, I noticed a ditch there. So I poured the bucket of waste down into the ditch.

Afterwards, I went out into the fields to play with the other children, when we heard screams coming from the house. They were calling for us. When we got there, Aunt Rosa asked, "Who poured that bucket down into the ditch?" I said real low, "I did." Suddenly, Aunt Joan came rushing from the back of the crowd out of no where, "YOU DID WHAT?" "I did," I said softly. She grabbed me by the arm and took me into the house where she screamed and screamed and screamed. I kept crying and wishing so badly that I was back at home in Detroit. As I cried, I remember Aunt Emma coming into the room and saying something to Joan under her breathe. I never knew what it was, but she left me alone then. For the rest of my stay there, I avoided looking at Joan because I didn't want to see her hateful face. And sometimes when I walked by her, I could hear her mumbling very lowly, "I should whip your behind good."

When Jeannie conveyed that story to me, I cradled her in my arms and said, "I'm so sorry." After writing about Jeannie's story, I had not noticed that my son, David, who usually acts tough, was paying close attention to me as I read the story to someone else. To my amazement, David was crying so hard, he was shaking. When I asked him what was wrong, he did not respond. Then I asked, "Are you crying because of what happened to Jeannie?" He said, "Yes." I knew that I had to do some damage control immediately. Therefore, I stressed the importance of forgiveness and the way his dad would have wanted him to act toward his aunt. After I talked with him, he calmed down. He never mentioned it again; and I never talked about that topic in his presence. David's Aunt Joan was not well at the time. Recently, he said to me, "It is not important what happened in the past. It is important that I'm there to help her if she needs me." I thanked God. I did not want to be held responsible for his resentment of anyone.

CHAPTER 12

CHAPTER 12

After teaching for a few years, I returned to Wayne State University to pursue a Masters Degree in Education. I majored in Guidance and Counseling. I thoroughly enjoyed that area of study. Since I was working, I attended college part time. Finally, graduation was upon us. Although my husband was not there when I received my high school diploma, Associate Degree, and Bachelors, friends thought he would be there when I received my Masters Degree. I asked him to attend the commencement, but he refused. He offered me a gift of fifty dollars. However, I refused to take it. I was not going to allow my spouse to soothe his conscience with fifty dollars. Other members of my family attended my graduation. So I was not alone. Graduation was such a grand occasion. A former student teacher of mine was graduating and receiving his Bachelors Degree that night.

I took the necessary steps to get my name on the counselors' list. There was no counseling position available at my school, and I did not want to go to another school. I was given an opportunity to substitute in a counselor's place twice when he was ill. I enjoyed the experience. However, I missed that classroom interaction with my students. Therefore, I decided that I would not leave the classroom. My friends did not under- stand my decision. They thought I should have seized the opportunity to get out of the classroom. Their opinion did not bother me because by that time, I realized that success is not measured by making more money, or having a little more prestige attached to your name. Success is being happy doing what you're doing. Teaching students and training student teachers are among the great fulfillments of my life. Whenever I would see the knowledge which I conveyed to students surface through their performance, and behavior, I'd know that the seed of knowledge had taken root, and students were reaping the benefits. My teaching was not limited to English and Speech. I also gave instructions pertaining to life. When the opportunity presented itself, I informed them of the goodness of God. I taught students to beware of "self fulfilling prophecy." I told them to never live down to anyone's negative prediction of them. Whenever students laughed at how cheaply another student was dressed, I stressed the importance of "delayed gratification," the importance of making a sacrifice now for a better life later. If a student tries to have the expensive material things now, he/she may not remain focused on his/her goal in life. There were times when some students would poke fun at another student because he/she was on welfare. I would tell them that there was nothing wrong with being on welfare if you are working towards getting off of aid. I told my students that I was once on welfare. My sister said, "I would not have told them that." But I shared that information about my past with them because I wanted them to know that they could make it against the odds. I wanted them to understand that their present financial condition was not as important as their goals, their destination in life.

One of my most gratifying moments as an educator was when I received a letter from a young man who had just finished eleventh grade English in my class. In his letter he wrote, "Mrs. Sloan, when I first came into your room, I thought you treated me unfairly. However, I now realized that I am a better person because of the way you treated me. You not only taught me a lot about English. You taught me a lot about life. I waited until all students' grades were in before giving you this letter because I did not want you to think I was trying to get a better grade." The letter was signed, "Andre." Imparting my knowledge and experiences to my student teachers were equally important to me. I know that each teacher develops his/her own style of teaching. But when I'd see my instructions, ideas or values emerge from a student teacher, I'd have such a feeling of accomplishment. I knew that the seed of knowledge which I had planted, had taken root, surfaced, and was spreading. Most importantly, students were the beneficiaries. I thought of teaching as more than a career. I considered it my calling in life.

CHAPTER 13

Chapter 13

In March, 1989, we lost Uncle Curtis after a brief illness. For many years, he had been Mother's only surviving brother, and the uncle with whom we lived while we were growing up. We were saddened by his death. Uncle Curtis was sort of a father figure for my sisters and me after Daddy left us. Although he did not contribute to our financial needs, he was there to discipline us when necessary. We called him "Uncle Kurt." He was a nice looking dark brown skin man of medium height and build. He was Mother's youngest sibling. Uncle Kurt had a handicap which Mama Lillie blamed herself for. When Mama was pregnant with my uncle, she and her sister, Aunt Lessis, laughed and made fun of a lady who was crippled in one foot. When Uncle Kurt was born, he was crippled just like that lady. There was a difference, however. He was crippled in both feet. His feet were turned inward and curled in a ball like manner. He walked on the sides of his feet. He wore high top, lace up shoes all of his life. He could not walk with bare feet. If he had no shoes on, he had to crawl. Although Uncle Kurt was able to work, have a family and live a normal life, Mama Lille never seemed to forgive herself for his handicap. The moral of this story has taught me that one should never laugh at another person's misfortune.

During the summer of that year, Mona, Lila and I went to Warrington for a family reunion. We had a good time. Even though Lila was a diabetic on insulin, she ate anything she desired, much of which was not good for her. However, she seemed to have been okay. When we returned to Detroit, I went to see my doctor for a check-up. I felt all right. I just kept my appointment. My doctor informed me that my blood pressure was high and my E. K. G. was abnormal. After a short time, I was okay. Fall came, and Uncle Lonnie died. He was Daddy's brother who lived with us for quite some time after Daddy had abandoned us. It was he who offered to help Mother take care of us financially. Shortly after Lonnie's funeral, winter set in, and the holiday season was upon us. Lila was living alone then; and her health was not good. She asked to borrow eighty-four dollars from me, in order to purchase the groceries she needed for the holiday. She promised to repay me when she got her pay check within a few days. Her life was hard financially. I knew that I had more money than I would spend during the holidays. I loaned her eighty-five dollars. The check she was expecting from her employer, was for eighty-four dollars. How could I take her last dollars when I did not even need it? Yet I knew she would insist on paying the money back because she was a proud lady with integrity. So I hit upon something that was acceptable for both of us. I said to Lila, "Pay me back next summer, when I'm not teaching. I'll need it more then." She agreed to do so. That was the Christmas season of 1989. I had no way of knowing that would be our last Christmas together.

On Sunday morning, December 31, 1989, Lila telephoned me to ask if I were going to church. I told her that I wasn't going to morning service. I said I would go that night, which was New Years Eve watch service. So Lila did not go either. She called me again that night and asked if I was going to church. I said, "No." Lila said "I think I had better go." So she was at church when the New Year, 1990 came in. On the evening of January 1, 1990, Lila's daughter, Elaine, called to inform me that her mother, who was visiting a friend on the far east side of town at the time had been taken to the hospital by E. M. S. Close members of the family rushed to the hospital to be with her. Lila had gone into cardiac arrest, and was on life support. As she lay there looking as if she was sleeping, part of her body had gotten cold already. I felt as if we were living in a bad dream. Yet I knew what was happening was reality. As we sat in the CCU waiting room, I listened as Mother questioned the doctor about Lila's chance of survival. Finally, he said she had a 5% chance of survival. Mona and I waited for Mother to say to us "Lila is going to be all right." Mother had such a close relationship with God. We thought that she would be okay if Mother had been assured of it. However, those comforting words never came from her. About 2 or 3 O'clock the next morning, Mother, Mona and I went home. Lila's husband and daughters stayed at the hospital. Lila's clothing were sent home with me. That evening, Mona and I returned to the hospital. Lila went into cardiac arrest again and died that evening. I can't begin to express my feelings that day. I've always cried more easily than any of Mother's children. However, the tears backed up that day and would not come. Mona returned to work as a means of keeping her mind occupied with other things. I took off work and went about the business of helping my brother-in-law and nieces make funeral arrangements. After the funeral, numbness was replaced by grief. Then I cried for the sister who had my back for as long as I could remember.

When we were growing up, we played together, fought each other, clowned around, laughed and cried together. Later, we went on double dates and shared many secrets. She was my protector. When we attended school together, there were many girls who wanted to beat me up. I would take on those girls who were my own size. Lila insisted on taking on the big girls herself. I have seen her fight girls who looked like big football players, for my sake. Whenever there was a disagreement between someone else and me, I never had to wonder whose side she would take. She always had my back. Lila was one of the most loyal, supportive people I have ever known. Of course one other thing that bound Lila and me together was the fact that older members from Mother's side of the family made a difference between Mona, Lila and me. Lila and I got the short end of the stick. After Lila died, I said to Mother, "I always felt as though Lila and I stood on one side, and the rest of the family was on the other side. Now, I feel as if I am standing all alone." I think those words elicited compassion from Mother. She and I became closer. My relationship with God, and my work helped to ease the pain of grief after Lila's death. Thus I was able to get a grip, and carry on.

CHAPTER 14

CHAPTER 14

During the summer of 1990, the Winston Family Reunion was hosted in Detroit. The Winston's are relatives on my mother's side of the family. The reunion was very nice; even though that was the first one without Lila by my side. Life was so empty without her around. That winter, my stepfather, whom we called "Mr Sam," was diagnosed as having prostate cancer. Although he made no attempt to be close to us when we were growing up, he was still important to us because he was there. I remember how faithful Mr. Sam was when I was in college. During the first two years of college, when I had no other means of transportation, he would always be there to pick me up at night after classes were over. For two semesters, when I had to take classes that were only taught early during the day, my stepfather would come to my home and babysit Shawny, who was just a toddler at the time. Beau and David were unable to babysit because they were at school. I told him that I would remember him when I graduated. I kept my promise. Occasionally, I would go to Mother's house and give both Mother and my stepfather money. They did not have to ask for it; neither did there have to be a special occasion. As time passed, his illness caused him to dwindle from a big robust man to an extremely small man.

The summer of 1991 was upon us. My husband's family reunion was being held in another state. Unfortunately, Phil could not attend because his doctor had requested that tests be run on him to determine his physical condition, Since my husband did not share information with me, I learned about the tests by listening to him converse with other people. He refused to discuss the topic with me. So the summer went by, and I had no idea what was happening pertaining to my husband's physical condition. During the fall of 1991, Ford employees were off work for two weeks, due to the change-over. Phil spent the entire two weeks in bed. That was not characteristic of him. I also noticed that he had begun to lose weight. Whenever I'd ask him how he felt, or what the tests results were, he would become angry and tell me to go on downstairs. I would then become irritated and leave him alone. Eventually I would seek answers again, but I always got a negative response from him. Thus I remained in the dark about his physical condition. As I was cleaning the bathroom one night during the beginning of December, I picked up a piece of paper from the bathroom floor to put into the waste basket. Before throwing the paper away, I decided to read it. It was a doctor's excuse stating when Phil would be able to return to work. The doctor's excuse stated, "It is suspected that he has metastatic disease." I didn't know what the word "metastatic" meant. Therefore, I called my sister and asked her to look up the definition in her medical dictionary. Mona informed me that it meant cancer. I was shocked and hurt. I telephoned some member of my husband's family so that his relatives would be informed. Uncle Shelly came to pick Phil up and take him to his doctor, Dr. Harth. My husband was referred to a urologist. After the examination, the urologist bluntly stated to Phil "You have prostate cancer, and I can't cure it." I felt that the doctor should have been a bit more sensitive to my husband's feelings. As my brother-in-law drove Phil, his sister, Joan, and me home, there was very little conversing between us. I guess we were in a state of shock. It was as if a hush had fallen over the four of us.

After that, Phil and I could discuss his illness without his becoming angry. He no longer stayed in seclusion in our bedroom anymore. Dr. Harth kept me abreast of what was going on. I learned that Phil's cancer was in its fourth and final stage. It had already reached the bone. There were treatments, however. My husband anxiously began those treatments. I decided to have Christmas dinner at our house that year and invite Phil's family. I thought that might make him happy. I felt that I had all the necessities for the family dinner except one thing. We desperately needed more silverware. I could not afford to buy a new set. I thought of the beautiful, unique, goldplated flatware set that I had purchased from my sister about two years before. The designs on the set were exquisite. Lila told me the set was Egyptian. I had searched for that set for more than a year. Unfortunately, it was no place to be found in our home. Since my son, David, was a drug abuser at the time, I accused him of taking my flatware set to sell. However, David was consistent in denying that he had stolen the set, but I did not believe him. I could think of no one else who would have taken it. Shortly before the family dinner, I discussed our need for flatware, and the missing Egyptian set with my husband. I loved the flatware, not only because it was beautiful, but it was one of the last things I got from my sister, Lila, before she died. Then my husband shocked me by informing me that he had taken my set to his sister, Joan's home a long time before. I looked at him with both anger and shock. I could hardly believe that he had let his sister have my favorite flatware set. Although I tried not to argue with Phil anymore after he became ill, he must have sensed, from the expression on my face, what I was thinking, because he said, "I didn't have to tell you where it is." My husband then telephoned his sister and asked her if she still had the flatware. He asked her to bring it with her when she came to dinner. After he talked with Joan, I telephoned her to remind her to bring the set with her. I never mentioned it to Phil again. I avoided arguing with him after I learned of his illness. I felt that he already had enough to worry about. I thank God for making it possible for me to get my set back before my husband left. Otherwise, I would not have known where it was. Thus I would never have gotten my set back. However, God meant for the flatware to be returned to me. Phil's family members came from far and near. During the evening of the dinner, everyone tried to be cheerful. I thought we did a good job of cheering Phil up, until I looked at a tape of the event. There was a look of sadness on various faces. Although Phil's health was deteriorating, he was still able to drive where he wanted to go. He would visit my stepfather, who also had prostate cancer, and Aunt Estelle, who by that time, was very ill with nuclear palsey.

As my stepfather's condition became more grave, my son David, stayed by Mr. Sam's bed side both night and day. In June, 1992, my stepfather, the man who helped to raise me from the time I was ten years old, made his demise. We were saddened by his death. During July of that year, Phil traveled by train to a family reunion in Florida. He was accompanied by Jeannie, Shawny, and Brandy, our granddaughter. He especially wanted Brandy to accompany him. He adored all his grandchildren. He was able to converse with, and relate to his grandchildren. He developed a very positive rapport with them. I don't believe there was ever a grandfather who loved his grandchildren more than Phil loved his. Unfortunately, he never developed that kind of relationship with his children. He worked hard and provided well materially, for his children. He just did not give them himself. Our children longed for a relationship with their dad. Nevertheless, they all loved him. Perhaps he considered it weakness for a man to show affection.

Later that summer, my friend Odessa, her husband, Isaac, her sister, Diane, and friends came to Detroit. I invited them for dinner in our home. Odessa and I had been friends since we were both fourteen years old. We had been married for many years. Yet our husbands had never met. I'm glad that Phil and Isaac finally met. We had a lovely evening with our friends from Tennessee. During the months that followed, Phil's condition grew worse. He spent a lot of time in and out of the hospital. Just before Christmas of 1992, one of his doctors said to me, "Make this the best Christmas ever for him; and if you have any children out of town, tell them to get in here!" I watched my husband go from a strong, vibrant, healthy man, to helpless. I can only imagine how that must have bothered him because he was so accustomed to being in control. Our twenty-four year old daughter, Shawny, lived with us. She took very good care of him when I was at work. She was so patient with him, he advised her to pursue a career in nursing. Finally, Phil's doctor recommended HOSPICS for him. Members from that health care organization came to our home to discuss what their organization entailed. My husband signed for their help. Although I could have gotten more physical assistance from HOSPICS, I could never accept that for Phil. I learned that the organization was for patients with a life expectancy of six months, more or less. It was stressed that they would make a patient as comfortable as possible while awaiting death. However, I wanted all medical assistance possible to be given to Phil during the time of crisis. Therefore, Shawny and I, with the assistance of another home health care organization, took care of him. Thus I was able to take him to the hospital emergency whenever a real crisis occurred. Each time he was taken to emergency, he was always admitted to the hospital.

Eventually, Phil became unable to walk. Although he must have been in terrible pain, he never said so. I only knew he was in pain when he asked for pain pills. I never heard him groan, or complain about pain. He took his discomfort like a champion. During the last few months of Phil's life, neither he nor I could sleep very well at night. Once he told me that there seemed to have been 48 hours in a day. Sometimes I would just lie in bed, awake all night, until it was time to get up and get ready for work the next morning. Although Phil's illness became worse, there were three things he still enjoyed: good food, counting his money, and listening to spiritual songs. I was reminded of how he used to play those songs on his guitar. My husband was the best guitar player I've ever known. By then, he was no longer able to play his guitar. The two good things that resulted from his illness, were that he sought the Lord and returned to church. Phil's daughter, Beatrice, and I developed a closer relationship also. Finally, Phil began to converse more with me. He was still however, easily irritated with me. I attributed much of his attitude to his illness. Therefore, I did not argue with him anymore. During that time, I longed for an apology, and an explanation of past mistreatment. It bothered me that during 36 years of marriage, we never celebrated an anniversary, and Mothers Day was ignored by my husband. He never went on a family outing with the children and me. It bothered me that he never accompanied me to church for our babies' christening. I used to feel so badly walking down the isle to have our babies christened, without my husband. As I walked down the isle toward the alter with each baby, I looked neither to the left, nor to the right because I did not want to see pity on the faces of others. I thought that somehow, with an apology, those issues could be put to rest. However, the apology never came. Since we seldom conversed, and I never heard him say anything positive about me, I knew that even after 36 years of marriage, he never knew the inner me. We were then coming down to the wire, and far too many issues were unresolved.

On the evening of November 15, 1993, I took Phil to the hospital for the last time. The doctor said to me, "Your husband is trying to die. He might die tonight." I heard those words, but I guess I was somewhat in denial. You see, Phil had had many close calls before, but he always survived. As I stood beside his hospital bed that night, I said to him, "I love you, and I know you love me." He said weakly, "Uh, huh." I was not really sure of his love, but I felt the need that night to assure him that I was confident of his love. Well, Phil made it through the night. About seven o'clock the next morning, while my husband was sleeping, I went home to get a nap and change clothing. I told my son to awake me at a certain time so I could go back to the hospital. His sister, Joan, was with him when I left. She went home about nine o'clock that morning. While I was asleep, about mid day, there was a call from the hospital informing me that Phil had taken a turn for the worse. I thought he had passed away, and they did not want to inform me by phone. I remember being extremely nervous, but I did not cry. I asked my sister to go to the hospital with me. I telephoned Joan. She was very upset. Since she had worked in the medical field herself, she knew what that message from the hospital meant.

Sure enough, when we arrived at the hospital during the early afternoon of November 16, my husband had made his demise. Although I had cried many times before his death, on that day, the tears backed up. I don't remember crying until the funeral was over. After about a week, I returned to work. My work kept my mind occupied with other things during the day. However, I was still unable to sleep at night, just as I was before Phil's death. I would lie awake until it was time to get ready for work. The nights seemed extremely long. I thought of how Phil had suffered. I remembered watching him go through four of the five stages of death and dying. I watched him go through denial, anger, depression and bargaining. I never saw him go through the last stage, which is acceptance.

For a long time after my husband's death, I appeared to have been doing fine outwardly. However, I was quite troubled within. You see, when Phil died, there were so many unresolved issues. In addition to grieving because of the loss of my husband, I grieved for what might have been. Time for our marriage had run out, and the clock could never be turned back. I could not understand why Phil refused to take me to and from church when I could not drive or had no car. During the first several years of our marriage, I had to depend on various members of my family for transportation. I could not understand why he would not take our son, Lyle, to the hospital emergency when Lyle had been ill for a few days, and his condition had grown worse. It was my stepfather who came to take us to the hospital. Phil made no attempt to drive us, even then. Once when Beau, our eldest son, was about 9 years old, he and other kids were playing in our back yard. The den windows opened outwardly. Somehow he got in the way of the sharp pointed edge of one of those windows. The cut in the top of Beau's head bled profusely. Phil was right there. He saw what was happening, but refused to take our son to the hospital emergency. I telephoned my sister. It was my brother-in-law who came and took Beau and me to the hospital. Phil sat there and allowed someone else to take his son to the hospital. He did not seem embarrassed, nor did he make any excuses for his action. I'm glad I took Beau to emergency. His skull was not punctured, but eight stitches were taken in his head. I did not understand Phil's means of awakening me one morning. You see, he usually woke up before me each morning. Once I asked him to awake me at a specific time. And so he did. The next morning, he kicked me to wake me up. I was baffled by such contempt. We never did resolve any of these issues. Our wedded time has expired. Oh, that I had met today, at the dawning of yesterday.

Soon after Phil's death, a new problem arose. During the week after I buried my husband, my son, David, disappeared. No one I knew, had seen or heard from him. When Dave did not show up for either of the major holidays, the family thought he may have met with foul play. My sister, Mona, had her children checking periodically to see if a body fitting Dave's description had turned up at the city morgue. During the next few months, I would sometimes get choked up when I thought about my missing son. Whenever I was near tears, God encouraged me. A voice would speak to me, saying, "Don't worry about David. God is working it out." Then the spirit beared witness. Thus immediately, my tears would back up. I reasoned that God was not encouraging me like that for nothing. My son was either still alive; or if he was dead, he died a saved man, and I would meet him in Glory. Therefore, I was able to get a grip and carry on. My children were planning a birthday party for me on May 1. Shortly before my birthday, Shawny asked, "Mom, what do you want for a gift?" I answered chokingly, "My son." During the last week of April, Dave came home. That led to the happiest birthday celebration of my life.

CHAPTER 15

Chapter 15

Aunt Estelle was still suffering from nuclear palsey. Her condition had gotten progressively worse. She could barely talk, and could not focus well enough to read or write. My aunt had always seemed so strong and vibrant. Uncle Shelly tried to take care of her, but he was ill himself. This aunt and uncle had helped to carry us financially, during the years we were growing up. The time had come for Mother to help take care of her younger sister. Mona and her husband helped a lot. I helped also; but Mother spent days at a time there taking care of her sister. During the summer of 1996, Mona, her husband and I traveled to Chicago. While we were there, Mother had my son, Dave, telephone us. He said that Aunt Estelle had gone back to the hospital, and Mother did not expect her to return home again. When we returned to Detroit, Mona and I went to visit our aunt in the hospital. She was scheduled to have surgery on the following day. However, my faithful aunt died before going into surgery. After Aunt Estelle's funeral, Uncle Shelly tried to continue living alone in his home. Unfortunately, his condition had gotten progressively worse. He then went to live with a member of his family. Ten months after my aunt's death, my uncle made his demise.

Although the loss of many love ones saddened me, I never lost sight of my blessings. I still had God, many other family members, and my best friend Jackie, whom my children refer to as "my sister." Throughout most of my career as a teacher, Jackie has always been there for my family and me. She and I became friends the day I discovered that she had graduated from Lane College in my home town. Jackie and I worked together daily, teaching in the same department for many years.

Finally, the time came when I knew I would not work another entire year. Therefore, I groomed my student teacher to take over my job when I retired. We both hoped that the principal would allow her to do so. I planned to retire at the end of the first semester. When I informed my students of my plans to retire, they were crushed. Even students whom I had never taught, were unhappy about my leaving. One day a young man whom I did not know, came to my room and said, "You're Mrs. Sloan, aren't you?" I said, "Yes." The young man then said, "It's out all over school that you are retiring, and nobody is happy about it." It was gratifying to know that so many students cared. On my last day at school, students in each of my classes wrote comments on large cards for me. I could not hold back the tears as I read the comments of students. Therefore, I decided to finish reading them at home, with a box of kleenex nearby. The principal allowed my student teacher to fill my position. I was happy. Therefore, my students did not have to adjust to a stranger for a teacher during the middle of the school year. I knew they were in good hands. Ms. Khraizat is a very caring, competent teacher. On February 1, 1999, I officially retired from the Detroit School System. Thus, I stepped away from my career as a teacher, and embarked upon a new phase of my life.

Jackie, along with the rest of the English Department and friends, planned a grand retirement party for me. It was classy elegance with the common touch. It was also a reunion. Friends who had left my school many years before, came to help me celebrate. Some of my former students, Alanda & Kelly, whom I taught during the late 1970s were there. Alanda is now married to my nephew. Kelly sang one of my favorite songs, "Wind Beneath My Wings." Several members of my family were there to hear all of the wonderful comments and poetry readings about me. Serena, my favorite former student teacher was also there. Serena is special to me because she took my instructions, my advice more to heart than any of my other student teachers did. She is like a daughter, following in my footsteps. Jackie, who is great at writing fiction, wrote a story about my life in which she compared my plight into the world of academics, to Harriett Tubman's plight into the world of freedom. We had great fun. My retirement party was held at one of Detroit's finest restaurants. I shall always remember and be grateful for my retirement celebration. I now realize that no matter where I find myself in life, I shall always be a teacher at heart. My philosophy of education is to convey the knowledge which I have acquired, to students in a manner that stimulates interest and enhances comprehension. Recently, my friend Jackie, paid me a surprising compliment. She said "Perserverance, you are a hero." I did not tell Jackie that she, along with my good friends Mary, Odessa, Carolyn and Angela, have contributed to the total sum of me.

CHAPTER 16

Chapter 16

On July 10, 1999, I had a dream that disturbed me. I dreamed that Aunt Estelle, who had been dead for almost three years, came back, and I had to go back with her. I did not want to leave this earth, but I had no choice. As we were departing, going toward Heaven, I looked back at a woman who stood in front of a house on earth, and said to her "Thank you for raising me." We then continued to travel upward. As we went upward, I went through what appeared to have been electrical wires. I felt absolutely nothing. Therefore, I assumed that it was not my body traveling upward. Even though we were going in the right direction, I did not want to leave this earth. I had the dream on Saturday morning. I know that many dreams don't mean anything. However, some do have meaning. So I asked my sister to pray for me. The next day, Mona and I went to church. Mother had an arthritic problem which prevented her from attending church regularly as she used to. She lived near church. So she would sit on her front porch and watch for Mona and me. We would stop by her house after service was over and tell her about the message. Before leaving Mother's home that Sunday evening, I told her about the dream I had on the previous day. I asked her to pray and ask the Lord to give me more time here, if the dream did have meaning. Mother listened as she sat there on her porch, but said nothing in response to my dream. As we were leaving her house that Sunday evening, I reminded her to pray for me. She responded to my request by saying "You all keep me praying." That was the last time I ever saw my mother alive. On Monday, the next evening, Monica, my niece who lived with Mother, called to tell me that my mother didn't seem to be feeling well. Monica informed me that she was going to call E. M. S. My sister and brother-in-law arrived first. Then David and I arrived at Mother's home. When we got there, Mother was gone. I was shocked and hurt, as a great sense of loss flooded over me like a river. You see, Mother had always been a human anchor and refuge for her children, grandchildren, and many others. When Mother was pronounced dead, I cried while embracing Mona, and asked, "What are we going to do?" My sister responded "We're going to make it!" I was fully aware that I had lost the best friend I had and ever will have on this earth. I had loved and respected her, confided in, and trusted her all of my life. She never once failed me.

During the days that followed, I would break down and cry each morning when I awoke and remembered that Mother was gone. My daughter, Shawny, would comfort me as I bent over crying. My greatest source of comfort came from the Lord. Many mornings, as I began to cry, a voice would speak to me and say, "She's gone to Glory!" Then immediately my tears would back up. I realized that Mother was in a far better place. I was just feeling sorry for myself. I shall always be grateful that she did not suffer. She had a heart attack that evening and was gone. Monica told me that Mother was speaking in tongue, talking to God as she was departing this life. I thought "What a beautiful way to leave this plain!" As I looked down on Mother's remains, my mind flashed back to my childhood. I remembered that when I was a sick little girl, Mother took me with her to the home of the white folks for whom she worked, so that she could keep an eye on my condition all day. Since we were too poor to have a telephone most of the time, Mother could not call my grandmother to check on my condition. Therefore, she took me to work with her. I remembered being in extreme pain when I was very young. The doctor said I had spots on my liver. The older I got, the more intense the pain became. I would be on my knees on the floor with excruciating pain in my stomach. Once when I was about 9 years old, I was in great pain while Mother ironed my slip for me to wear to the doctor. She began to pray for God to heal me. She said she believed strongly that God would heal me. So she discontinued ironing my slip, and did not take me to the doctor. As a result of Mother's faith, I never had a problem with that condition again. The Lord healed me that day. I never heard Mother raise her voice, nor have I ever known her to show much anger. Yet she demanded and received great respect from us. She was a wonderful role model. I feel so honored, and so blessed to have had her for a mother. I was reminded that from the time I was very young until shortly before she died, Mother would say to me "I just want to take you by your hand and run with you." I never asked Mother what she meant by that statement. I always knew that statement had spiritual meaning. Evidently, Mother saw something within me which she deemed worthy.

I was reminded that after Daddy left us and went to live with Karmen and their new baby, Mother's family helped her financially. Had it not been for Aunt Estelle, Uncle Shelly and a few other relatives, I don't know how we would have survived. Aunt Estelle and Uncle Shelly provided a roof over our heads, furniture, and sometimes food to eat when we were little girls living in Tennessee. Some of Mother's cousins, who lived in Detroit at the time, heard of our difficulties. Cousin Ivory and his wife, Dell, offered to raise Lila. Cousin Lovie offered to raise me. However, Mother chose to keep us together, and do the best she could. Thank God, we made it! I remembered how intelligent she was. One would have to have been perceptive to realize it. People with surface minds would fail to appreciate her for the intellectual she was, because she was a woman of humility who was low keyed. Mother was a thinker, a poet, and a terrific writer. She evoked within me a desire to think and to reach out beyond myself. Once she said to me, "What is the difference between knowledge and wisdom?" After thinking for a few seconds, I said "Knowledge is information which we acquire. Wisdom is knowing how to apply that acquired knowledge." Mother replied, "That's right." I hold a degree in Speech Communication, and I have given many effective speeches. Yet it was Mother who researched and gleaned information for some of those speeches. She literally wrote a few speeches for me. I put my little spin on them, gave a good oral delivery and walked away with all the credit. Mother was just proud of my accomplishments. She truly was the "wind beneath my wings."

Mother taught my siblings and me to overcome obstacles that seemed insurmountable. She encouraged us to view trouble as an opportunity to strengthen our character and draw closer to God. I am so grateful for the values she instilled. The greatest gift she gave us is a Christian Heritage. We shall never allow her teaching to die. It will be passed down as a legacy, from generation to generation. While looking down on Mother's remains, I was reminded of her kindness and generosity to others. They did not have to be relatives or friends. She would reach out to help anyone who was in need. If one asked for money, and she only had two dollars, she would give half of what she had. If she believed that the other person's need was greater than her own, Mother would give all that she had. Mona said that Mother was the kindest person she has ever known. I agree with my sister completely. Even though my mother was 87 years old when she made her demise, there were many young people who attended her funeral. Shawny told me that a few of them looked like drug addicts who had cleaned themselves up and had come to church to say good-bye to Mother. I understood why. They were all young people whose lives were touched by Mother in a positive way. During her latter years, my son, David, spent more time with my mother than any of her other grandchildren. Mother told me how she prayed for Dave to be delivered from drug abuse. I hope that somehow, she knows that Dave no longer uses drugs. He has come out of the streets. He has gotten saved and attends church. I feel so blessed to have had her for a mother. I believe that each person whose life she touched, would agree that life is more meaningful, and the world a little brighter for having known her. I know that I shall never meet anyone like unto my mother again. I am most blessed.

As I stood there looking down on Mother's remains, I remembered that she had shared something with me which the Lord had given her pertaining to getting rid of the hiccup. I found the information to be true. Therefore, over a period of almost twenty years, I shared it with a few thousand students. Whenever someone in my classroom would have the hiccup, I would say to him/her, "Go across the hall to the water fountain, and drink three swallows of water. Drink the first swallow in the name of the Father, the second swallow in the name of the Son, and the third swallow in the name of the Holy Ghost." I told the student, in the presence of the rest of the class, "If you do that, the hiccup will go!" So students did as I told them, and the hiccup left instantly. Only one student came back and told me that he still had the hiccup. I said to him, "You've got to have faith." He went back a second time and got rid of his hiccup. Once a young lady in one of my tenth grade classes, told me that her mother said I was playing with God. I replied, "Tell your mother that my mother lives close to God. The Lord gave this to her, and she shared it with me." Then something happened that I did not expect. A young lady who had been a real problem to me in the classroom, got out of her seat, walked across the room, and said to the class, "It works!" Of course no student was encouraged to follow my suggestion if he/she did not want to do so. I shared this information with my students over the years as a means of enabling them to get rid of the hiccup; but most of all, I wanted them to grasp faith, and acknowledge the power of God. So through me, Mother's informational gift from God has reached thousands.

For as long as I can remember I never heard Mother bad-mouth people or put anyone down. If she knew that we were angry with someone, she would try to point out that person's positive qualities. I knew she was not being disloyal or naive. Her remarks were for our benefit. She knew that it was not good for us mentally, physically, or spiritually to dwell on anger or harbor resentment toward anyone. Mother truly was the most compassionate person I have ever known. Through the life Mother lived, and her teaching, she led so many people to the Lord. For years I have said, "I want to go to Heaven someday, but I don't want to go in empty handed. I want to be responsible for others making it in." Mother must have been responsible for a multitude of people giving their lives to God. She loved people; but most of all, she loved God. She used to say, "I been raised, and brought up by the Lord!" I have observed Mother's upright character all of my life. No one can spot her life. God bestowed a great honor upon me when he gave me her for a mother. She utilized her time well while on this earth. Just as God raised up Moses, Harriet Tubman, Rosa Parks, Martin Luther King Jr. and others for a special purpose in life, so did He raise up my mother. She made such a spiritual difference in the lives of so many people. Mother was an unsung hero. Finally, as I stood there looking down on her remains, I whispered, "Thank you Mother, for a job well done." Many months have passed since Mother left us. I shall always be grateful for the prayers she sent up for David in advance. Oh God, there is another storm approaching! Dave recently informed me that he has been diagnosed as having a terminal illness. His doctors have informed the family that David's death is inevitable. I know that even now, God is able to work a miracle. Whatever happens, I pray that God will strengthen me, and enable me to ride the waves of this storm until I can see the rainbow.

I will never regret my plight in life. I feel that I have had the best of both worlds. I know what it is like to be poverty stricken, downtrodden, disrespected and mistreated. Those things have caused me to be grateful to God for the days of sunshine in my life. I was given the strength and courage to persevere and overcome. My entire past has contributed to the total make up of me. Therefore, all of the negative and positive things that happened in my life, have contributed to the strength of my character. So with no regrets, and with my head held high, I step into tomorrow.